1

Table of Contents

I. The 50ᵗʰ Anniversary of the Equal Pay Act of 1963

A. Foreword

Fifty years ago, President John F. Kennedy signed landmark legislation to guarantee equal pay for women and men performing equal work for the same employer. The Equal Pay Act of 1963 was the first in a series of major federal and state laws that had a profound effect on job opportunities and earnings for women over the next half century, and laid the foundation for the movement of women into the paid labor force at unprecedented levels. The following year, another groundbreaking law passed: the Civil Rights Act of 1964 prohibited discrimination on the basis of sex, race, color, national origin, and religion. Further cementing workplace protections between 1965 and 1967, President Lyndon B. Johnson issued a series of Executive Orders designed to ensure non-discrimination among Federal contractors. These critical legal advances bolstered five decades of economic and social progress for women – but much more remains to be done.

Since passage of the Equal Pay Act, several generations of women have transformed our workplaces and, in turn, our economy. Women have integrated many previously exclusively male job fields, and have achieved success at the highest levels of many fields. Women have achieved higher levels of education than ever before, and now serve at the highest levels of government, the judiciary, in Congress, and in private industry. They have become important sources of job creation, entrepreneurship, and innovation.

This progress notwithstanding, in 2011, the average woman still earned only 77 cents for every dollar earned by men.[1] Moreover, women continue to comprise a majority of employees in many low-wage sectors. For example, in 2012, fifty-two percent of all women in the full-time labor force worked in service, sales and office occupations, such as secretaries, cashiers, retail sales persons, maids, child care workers and customer service representatives, and comprised an overwhelming majority of the workers[2] in each of those sectors.

These sobering statistics matter. Women comprise nearly half of our workforce, and many women are the primary breadwinners for their families. Their level of earnings drive essential economic decisions – including decisions about quality of housing, access to medical treatment, educational attainment for children, child care, clothing, and food and other essentials. And of course, these earnings have a long-term effect on a woman's ability to save and prepare for retirement. When women are short-changed, their personal financial stability suffers, and their families suffer. But that is not all: women's lower earnings impact all levels and sectors of the economy, as well as local communities, since lower pay means fewer dollars are spent within neighborhood businesses or invested in new ventures. For these reasons, equal pay is important for our nation, the broader economic security of our families, and the growth of the middle class in our economy.

Fifty years ago, Congress and the President recognized that the Equal Pay Act was the first step to address overt sex-based compensation discrimination in employment that impeded women's ability to achieve workplace equality. The United States has made significant progress in widening the path to greater opportunities for women, but our work is not yet complete. With this report, we reaffirm our steadfast commitment to America and our national imperative of workplace equality for all.

The Task Force thanks the Council of Economic Advisors for their contributions to Part II of this report.

B. Introduction: The Evolution of Women's Economic Status Between 1963 and 2013

The Equal Pay Act established a basic labor standard requiring employers to pay women and men the same wages when performing jobs that are equal, or substantially equal, in content. It was the first national labor standard to address a widespread practice of paying women less simply because they were women, and it laid the foundation for future workforce policies. Other important legislation and policies soon followed, which helped broaden employment opportunities for women and strengthened their ability to challenge unlawful discrimination.

Fifty years after passage of the Act, major shifts in the socio-economic status of women have transformed our nation's workplaces, communities, and families. This report explores the increase of women in the paid labor force since passage of the Equal Pay Act, and the passage of laws that have expanded civil rights protections for women experiencing unlawful pay discrimination. The first part of this report contains an assessment of workforce trends in three timeframes: 1960-1980; 1980-2000; and the early years of the 21st Century, from 2000-2010. Using data on labor force participation, earnings, occupations, educational attainment and entrepreneurship, and available data examining the differences among women by race/ethnicity and age, this report describes the progress of women in the paid labor force since the passage of the Equal Pay Act. It also compares women's status in the workforce to that of men and analyzes the evolution of women's and men's roles in the workplace, community, and family.

After reviewing five decades of data, the report addresses the status of equal pay for women today, the pay gap and other persistent challenges that remain in light of the fact that continued momentum has stalled in recent years. In the final section entitled, "2010 and Beyond," the report reflects on the efforts of President Barack Obama's Administration to eliminate the pay gap and on the federal equal pay agenda moving forward.

The Equal Pay Act and the Decades of Civil Rights Legal Advances That Followed

One year after passing the Equal Pay Act, Congress enacted the Civil Rights Act of 1964, a sweeping federal ban on discrimination. Title VII of the Act banned employment discrimination on the basis of race, color, religion, national origin, and sex. One year later, Executive Order 11246 prohibited federal government contractors from discriminating in employment and required them to engage in affirmative action to ensure equal opportunity based on race, color, religion, and national origin. Noticeably absent was any prohibition based on sex. In 1967, Executive Order 11246 was amended by Executive Order 11375, which prohibited discrimination on the basis of sex in hiring and employment within the federal government. Additionally, Title IX of the Education Amendments of 1972 opened the doors for women to pursue education free from discrimination in those educational institutions that received federal financial assistance. The Pregnancy Discrimination Act of 1978 strengthened employment discrimination protections for women who were pregnant, gave birth, or had related medical conditions. And in the 1990s, the Civil Rights Act of 1991 and the Family and Medical Leave Act of 1993 provided further protections for American workers, including broadening workplace leave rights for men and women and beginning to address critical barriers to full economic equality that stem from medical conditions and care giving responsibilities.

Economic and Social Progress, But a Persistent Pay Gap Remains

Women have made significant progress since the passage of the Equal Pay Act. Women's labor force participation rate in 2012 was 57.7 percent, over fifty percent higher than it was in the early 1960s.[3] In 1960, roughly 15 percent of managers were women; by 2009, almost 40 percent of managers were women.[4] The ratio of women's to men's annual earnings has narrowed from 59 cents for every dollar paid to men in 1963, to 77 cents in 2011.[5] The educational progress of women, who now outnumber men in their attainment of Bachelor's Degrees, Master's Degrees and Doctoral Degrees,[6] has driven the gains in earning power. Yet today, 50 years after the Equal Pay Act became law, a pay gap still exists, and studies have demonstrated that a significant portion of the wage gap cannot be fully explained when controlling for factors such as labor market experience and job characteristics.

The movement of women into the entrepreneurial ranks has offered women new earning opportunities. According to the Economic Census, in 1972, 486,009 firms were owned by women, but by 1982, the number had exploded to 2,612,621 firms. In 1982, receipts of women-owned firms reached $101,856,490, and they employed 1,254,588 employees and had payroll costs of $11,561,025.[7] More recently, the 2007 Census Survey of Business Owners reported that women's business ownership accounted for over a quarter of all businesses nationwide and generated over $1.2 trillion in business receipts.[8] That same year, the number of employees working in women-owned firms reached 7.6 million, with nearly half (45.9 percent) of all women-owned businesses operating in repair and maintenance industries; personal and laundry services; health care and social assistance; and professional, scientific and technical services.[9]

Occupational Segregation and Other Barriers to Equality Remain

Although working women have made progress in many areas, the workforce continues to be characterized by occupational segregation of women and men into different types of jobs. In Part II, this report discusses the potential impact of occupational segregation on the pay gap and some of the ways federal agencies intend to tackle that problem going forward.

In 1960, nearly two-thirds of working women were employed in clerical, service or sales positions. Thirteen percent of women held professional jobs, but even these posts were likely to be traditional women's jobs such as nursing or teaching positions.[10] Indeed, even the classified section in newspapers listed jobs separately for men and for women, a practice that would persist into the next decade. As women's educational attainment increased during the 1980s and beyond, so did women's movement into higher-paying professional and management jobs, where women now compose 51.5 percent of employed workers.[11] However, even today, women still are much more likely to enter occupations where the majority of workers are female, including the healthcare, education and human services fields. In addition, over half of all women continue to be employed in lower-paying sales, service and administrative support positions. Despite substantial gains in the management fields, women still lag behind in other non-traditional fields such as transportation, construction, and the science, technology, engineering and mathematics (STEM) fields.[12]

In addition to gender differences in occupations, there are differences based on race and ethnicity, as well as differences for women who are mothers. For example, White and Asian women are more likely to work in higher-paying management, professional and related occupations than Black and Hispanic women, who are more likely to work in lower-paying service occupations and significantly more likely to be among the working poor.[13] And mothers of children under 18 years of age in 2011 had lower median weekly earnings compared to other women.[14]

The Pay Gap Narrows, But Not Enough

Over the last 50 years, the wage gap between women and men has closed by 17 percentage points. Women earned on average 59.8 percent of men's pay in 1963, and today, the wage ratio is 77 percent.[15] The narrowing of the wage gap reflects in part larger economic changes affecting men and families. For instance, a change in the wage gap results not only from a raise in women's real earnings (those adjusted for inflation), but also from a drop in real earnings for men since the mid-1970s.[16] Women's real earnings have increased by about 71 percent from $21,646 in 1960 to $37,118 in 2011, while men's earnings have increased at a significantly lower rate, 35 percent, from $35,675 in 1960 to $48,202 in 2011.[17] Major shifts in our economy over the last fifty years, particularly in the move from a manufacturing base to services, information and communications technologies, have changed the skills and education workers need to compete successfully in a global market.[18] These changes have not been easy for some workers to navigate as new skills and education requirements have become more important. These economic shifts have contributed to the transformed role of women in our nation's families.[19] Today, the wages of women, both as single parents and as co-breadwinners, are critical to the overall economic health and stability of a majority of the nation's families.[20]

Even as women made inroads into non-traditional higher-paying occupations, pay for women compared to men across most occupational categories reflects a wage gap, regardless of the gender composition of detailed occupations. The higher-paying supervisory and management positions manifest many of the largest pay differences.[21] This persistent wage gap, even among higher-paying professions, is a longstanding problem. In 1983, twenty years after the law began to require equal pay for equal work, female managers and administrators earned just 64 percent of the pay of male workers in these jobs.[22] In addition, women – particularly Black women, who traditionally have had higher labor force participation rates and more experience in the labor market than women of other race/ethnic groups – experienced difficulty advancing into leadership positions.[23] This persistent barrier to career advancement into the top tiers of management drew the attention of the public and is known popularly as "the Glass Ceiling." Highly educated and skilled women of all races and ethnicities began reporting resistance and outright discrimination that prevented them from moving into the higher ranks of management. In 2011, some of the greatest differences in the median weekly earnings of women and men occurred in the category of management occupations.[24]

The Way Forward

The 50-year economic, social and political history described in the next section of this report sets the stage for the choices and challenges we face today. While the law recognizes the basic right to equal pay for substantially equal work and freedom from wage discrimination, women's earnings still fall short of men's. Although a generation of political organizing and cultural change has eliminated many barriers, women still face challenges entering the most highly-paid occupations. And although our country's prosperity depends on women at every level – from the family budget to the national economy – we still cannot say we fully and fairly value their contributions. With that reality in mind, in the final section of this report, we turn to the policy, enforcement, education and outreach work federal agencies are implementing – and the plan going forward – to ensure that equal pay becomes a reality. We ask Congress to do its part by passing the Paycheck Fairness Act, and we identify the major steps we must take to close the pay gap once and for all. A half century after President Kennedy made a national commitment to the cause of equal pay, our work remains unfinished. Today, we renew our commitment to the principle of equality for all of America's workers.

C. Five Decades of Equal Pay History

1960-1980: A Time of Social, Political and Economic Transformation for Women

An Overview of the Political Climate and Legislative Developments

On June 10, 1963, President Kennedy gathered a group of influential women in the Oval Office as he signed the historic Equal Pay Act into law. Attending the ceremony were women and men who had championed the legislation and made the case for its urgency.[25] In signing the bill, President Kennedy stated:

> The lower the family income, the higher the probability that the mother must work. Today, 1 out of 5 of these working mothers has children under 3. Two out of 5 have children of school age. Among the remainder, about 50 percent have husbands who earn less than $5,000 a year – – many of them much less. I believe they bear the heaviest burden of any group in our Nation. Where the mother is the sole support of the family, she often must face the hard choice of either accepting public assistance or taking a position at a pay rate which averages less than two-thirds of the pay rate for men.[26]

While just over a third of all women were in the labor force in 1963,[27] the issue of pay discrimination was critically important to those working women and their families.

President Kennedy and advocates for the Equal Pay Act understood that the workforce was segregated greatly by gender and race. They also understood that, because the Act focuses on women and men working in the same occupations for the same employer, its reach would have limited benefits for the majority of women who did not work in jobs substantially the same as men's jobs. However, they saw the Act as an important first step.[28]

Despite its limitations, passage of the Equal Pay Act firmly supported women's economic rights and improved earnings. At the signing, President Kennedy explained that additional proposals to address the economic status of women were needed, and he fully expected his new Commission on the Status of Women, led by Eleanor Roosevelt and Assistant Labor Secretary Esther Peterson, to outline additional measures to boost the economic status of working women.

In October 1963, the Commission released *American Women: Report of the President's Commission on the Status of Women*. The report acknowledged the important, traditional roles of wife and mother. It also extensively documented the employment challenges women frequently faced when seeking employment and after becoming employed. These challenges included discriminatory practices that still resonate for women today – being denied employment and/or promotion, receiving unfair wages and fewer benefits, experiencing sexual harassment and workplace hostility, or facing discrimination on the basis of being pregnant.[29] These employment attitudes and actions impeded women's ability to obtain employment and advance in the workplace.

On the heels of the Commission's report, Congress passed and President Johnson signed the Civil Rights Act of 1964. In Title VII, the new law specifically addressed employment discrimination on the basis of race, color, religion, national origin, or sex. Sex was not originally among the prohibited bases of discrimination in the draft bill, but was inserted as an amendment during debate. When it passed with sex included, women gained a powerful new legal tool to fight workplace discrimination.[30]

An important factor in the tremendous changes in women's labor force participation, educational advancement, increased earnings and the role of mothers in the workforce over the last fifty years was the second wave of the U.S. women's movement. A growing political movement of women, including the leaders of traditional women's organizations, as well as new advocates who had been active in the civil rights movement, began visibly organizing. They recognized the need for a parallel political movement to challenge sex-based discrimination in a broad range of areas, including employment, housing, health care, access to credit, education, and child care.[31]

As increasing numbers of women became politically active and states formed their own commissions on the status of women, the call for more serious attention to discrimination against women grew louder.[32] In 1970, the Department of Labor issued sex discrimination guidelines interpreting Executive Order 11246 (prohibiting federal government contractors from discriminating in employment on the basis of race, color, religion, national origin and, because of the later amendment, sex) and addressed some of the more overt practices of discrimination and occupational segregation, such as advertising positions as "male help wanted" or "female help wanted."[33]

Equal pay rights expanded in 1972, with a series of key amendments to existing laws. Title IX of the Education Amendments of 1972, signed by President Richard M. Nixon, prohibited discrimination at educational institutions receiving federal funding. The prohibited discrimination included discrimination in rates of pay or any other form of compensation, and changes in compensation.[34] The 1972 Education Amendments also expanded the Equal Pay Act to cover executive, administrative, professional and outside sales employees.[35] In addition, in 1972, Congress strengthened Title VII by broadening its reach to public employers, educational institutions, and more private employers. As a result of these legislative changes, more women would have legal recourse for sex-based wage discrimination and other civil rights violations.

As the 1970s drew to a close, another significant piece of legislation for women — the Pregnancy Discrimination Act — was signed into law by President Jimmy Carter. This law amended Title VII of the Civil Rights Act to prohibit discrimination against pregnant workers, and to require that employers treat workers with pregnancy-related limitations the same way they treat other employees similar in their ability or inability to work.[36]

Increases in Women's Labor Force Participation and Educational Attainment

Against the backdrop of these laws that helped provide new employment and educational opportunities for women, and a growing socio-political movement, women began to enter the paid labor force in greater numbers and to seek higher levels of educational attainment. Women's labor force participation rate rose from 37.7 percent in 1960 to 43.3 percent in 1970, and to 51.5 percent by 1980.[37] The expansion of the overall female labor force largely reflected the influx of working mothers, whose labor force participation rates nearly doubled — from 27.6 percent in 1960 to 54.1 percent by 1980.[38]

Another noteworthy trend during this time was that, as the 1960s began, women's labor force participation rates varied greatly by race/ethnicity and marital and parental status. White women had a lower labor force participation rate than non-White women, but more specific data by race/ethnicity was not collected during this time.[39] Labor force statistics for Hispanic women were not collected by the Bureau of Labor Statistics until 1973; and, even then, the labor force participation rate for Hispanic women, hovering at 41 percent, was below that of Black and White women's participation rates, which were 49.8 and 44.1 percent, respectively. By 1980, the labor force participation rates of Black and White women were closer, at 53.1 and 51.2 percent respectively, while Hispanic women's labor force participation rate had climbed to 47.4 percent. Data for Asian women was not collected until 1990.[40]

For women with children, marital status also was a significant factor in labor force participation. When data on mothers by marital status first was collected in 1968, female single parents had a labor force participation rate of 61 percent, compared to 37 percent for married mothers. By 1980, female single parent participation rates had climbed to 68 percent while married mothers had increased their participation rates to 56 percent.[41]

Prior to 1980, the graphic representation of women's labor force participation rate by age resembled the letter "M," with a dip in women's participation during the prime child bearing and rearing years of ages 24-44. In contrast, men's graphic representation of labor force participation rates by age resembled an arc, and their participation reached its peak at ages 25-44. By 1980, the trend in greater labor force participation rates for women with children erased this graphical difference – so that the peak year of participation for women at ages 20-24 was followed by a slight decline by ages 25-34 and 35-54.

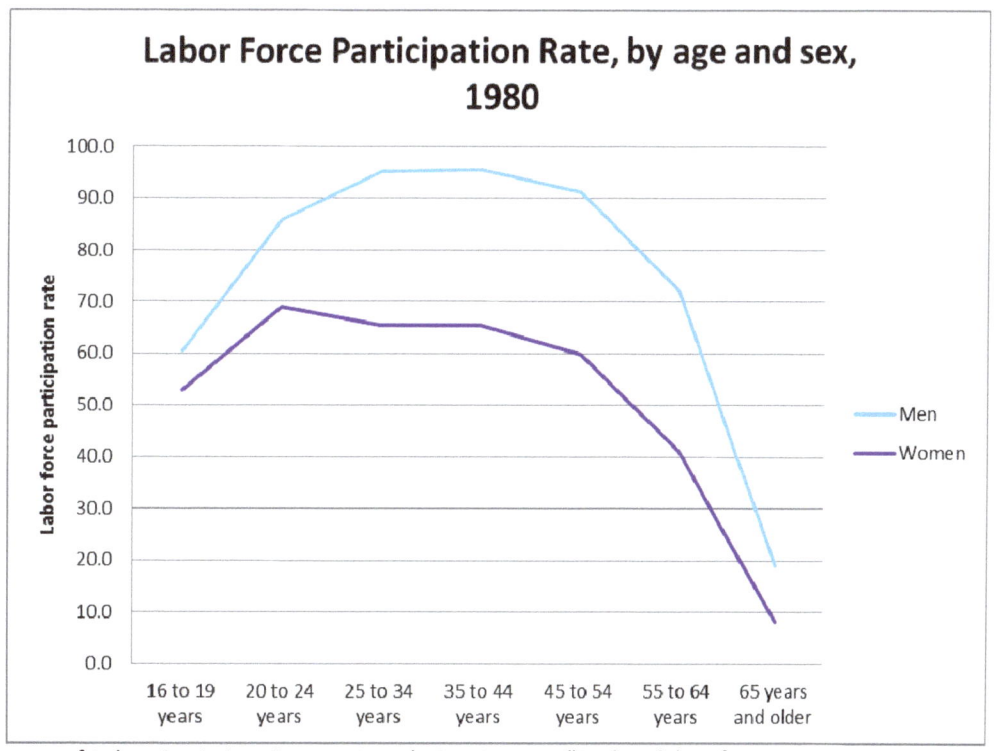

Source: Bureau of Labor Statistics, Current Population Survey. "Civilian labor force participation rates by age and sex, annual averages 1948-2012." (Unpublished table).

In addition to women's increased presence in the labor force, the 1960s-1980s witnessed a surge in the percentage of women obtaining Bachelor's, first professional and Master's Degrees. In 1960, only 35.3 percent of all Bachelor's Degrees were awarded to women, but by 1980, this figure had reached 49 percent. More dramatically, the proportion of first professional degrees awarded to women climbed from 3.6 percent in 1965 to 24.8 percent by 1980. Master's Degrees awarded to women climbed from 31.6 percent in 1960 to 49.2 by 1980.[42] The increase in women's educational attainment from 1960 to 1980 is one factor that contributed to a rise in earnings for women during the period. In contrast, real earnings for men increased greatly from 1960 and reached a peak in 1973, when they slowly began to fall through 1980.

By 1980, thanks to advances in women's educational attainment, the number of women in STEM fields began to increase – even though women still comprised 25 percent or less of the total employed in STEM occupations. By 1980, the most common non-traditional occupations for women included engineering and science technicians, computer specialists, physicians, dentists and related practitioners, as well as transport equipment operators, protective service and other positions on farms, handling stock or sales, or working as janitors.[43]

Top Ten Nontraditional Occupations for Women in Rank Order by Number of Women, 1960 and 1980		
Occupations	1960	1980
Farmers, managers, & tenant farmers	1	5
Farm laborers, wage workers	2	6
Accountants & auditors	3	
Janitors & sextons	4	2
Buyers and department heads, stores	5	
Stock clerks & storekeepers	6	
Salesmen & sales clerks, manufacturing	7	
Real estate agents & brokers	8	
Managers, food & dairy stores	9	
Postal clerks	10	
Nonfarm laborers -- stock handlers		3
Transport equipment operatives		1
Engineering & science technicians		4
Computer specialists		8
Protective service		7
Physicians, dentists, & related practitioners		9
Sales workers, except clerks, retail trade		10
Sources: Herman, A. M., & Castro, I. L. (1998). "Equal Pay: A Thirty-Five Year Perspective". Washington: U.S. Department of Labor. Page 19 - Table 2.		

The change in the wage gap during this time period reflects the broader changes in women's labor participation and educational attainment. In 1960, the women's to men's earnings ratio stood at 60.7 percent, and it widened over time as men's real earnings climbed faster and more dramatically than women's, reaching its widest point – 56.6 percent – in 1973. But by 1980, the earnings ratio was nearly back to where it was in 1960 – 60.2 percent.[44]

Early Enforcement of the Equal Pay Act

During the 1960s and 1970s, the Wage and Hour Division of the Department of Labor enforced the Equal Pay Act. By 1965, the Department already had recovered a total of $156,202 under the Equal Pay Act on behalf of 960 employees. Only a year later, the number of workers found to be underpaid had risen dramatically to 6,633 – due a total of $2,097,600 under the Equal Pay Act. By 1969, the number of workers found to be underpaid under the Act nearly tripled to 16,100 workers due $4,585,344.[45] By the end of 1978, the Department of Labor had recovered $162,063,460 for over 269,601 workers.

During this twenty-year period – thanks to cases filed by government agencies and private plaintiffs – federal courts established some key interpretations of the Equal Pay Act. In 1969, Associate Solicitor of Labor Bessie Margolin argued the first appeal of an Equal Pay Act case, *Schultz* v. *Wheaton Glass Company*, and successfully convinced the United States Court of Appeals for the Third Circuit that the Equal Pay Act only required jobs to be "substantially equal," not identical.[46] The case involved female "selector-packers" who were paid less than male "selector-packer-stackers." In 1974, in *Corning Glass v. Brennan*, the Supreme Court held that a wage differential arising "simply because men would not work at the low rates paid women" was illegal under the Equal Pay Act.[47] In 1979, enforcement of the Equal Pay Act was transferred from the Department of Labor and the Civil Service Commission to the U.S. Equal Employment Opportunity Commission (EEOC).[48]

1980-2000: Women Advance in the Emerging Information Age

An Overview of the Social, Economic and Political Climate

The last two decades of the 20th Century were marked by significant growth in the educational attainment of women, a narrowing of the wage gap between women and men, and resistance to the occupational segregation and workplace barriers that limited advancement opportunities for working women. In 1980, the wage ratio between women and men stood at 60.2 percent. Over the next two decades, the wage gap narrowed noticeably – reaching 71.6 percent by 1990, and 73.7 percent by 2000.[49]

The 1980s began with a focused strategy among the leaders in women's organizations and unions to raise women's pay and to clarify the differences between the Equal Pay Act and Title VII of the Civil Rights Act's prohibition against sex-based wage discrimination. In 1981, the Supreme Court ruled, in *County of Washington v. Gunther*,[50] that Title VII was not limited by the equal work standard found in the Equal Pay Act. Strengthened by this decision, many state and local coalitions of unions, women's and civil rights organizations worked together to challenge the lower pay given to women who worked in traditionally female-dominated occupations where few men were employed.

Over 20 states, a number of local governments and some private sector firms began conducting job evaluation studies, and some made wage adjustments to ensure that men and women working in different types of occupations, but with similar job evaluation scores, were paid comparable wages.[51] Much of this action was achieved through union negotiation and state or local legislation.

In addition to pay issues, working women frequently encountered outright sexual harassment and hostile workplaces. In 1980, the EEOC issued guidelines on sexual harassment, and the Supreme Court ultimately agreed in 1986 that Title VII's ban on sex discrimination in employment includes sexual harassment.[52] In 1991, Congress created the Glass Ceiling Commission to explore the challenges to women and people of color advancing in the labor force. In March 1995, the Commission issued *Good for Business: Making Full Use of the Nation's Human Capital,* a report documenting that women and minorities faced serious barriers to advancement to management and executive level positions. Further, where there were women and minorities in more senior positions, their compensation was lower than that of White males.[53]

In the 1990s, new federal laws ensured continued civil rights progress. Congress passed and President George H.W. Bush signed amendments to protect and expand Title VII following several Supreme Court decisions limiting its application. The Civil Rights Act of 1991 allowed Title VII plaintiffs, including those suing for intentional pay discrimination, to recover both compensatory and punitive damages subject to caps.

An additional barrier to the advancement of women in the workplace was lifted in 1993 when President William J. Clinton signed the Family and Medical Leave Act. This law provides eligible employees with up to 12 weeks of job-protected, unpaid leave for their own serious illness, that of their spouse, child or parent, and following the birth or adoption of a child. Employees are eligible for leave if they have worked for their employer at least 12 months, at least 1,250 hours over the past 12 months, and at a location where the company employs 50 or more employees within 75 miles.[54]

Soaring Educational Gains and Labor Force Participation Continue Through the End of the 20th Century

Women who were born in the wake of the Equal Pay Act, Title VII and Title IX of the Education Amendments Act came of age with a wide array of new educational and workforce opportunities. These young women achieved higher levels of education, while older women headed back to school, thus changing the male-to-female ratio at colleges across the United States. By 1981, women were earning half of all Bachelor's and Master's Degrees and over that decade gradually took the lead, earning 53 percent of all those degrees in 1990. This upward movement extended into the 1990s with women earning 57 percent of all Bachelor's Degrees and 58 percent of all Master's Degrees in 2000.[55] With regard to first professional degrees, women earned 25 percent of such degrees in 1980, 38 percent in 1990, and 45 percent by 2000. Among those seeking Doctoral Degrees, women earned 30 percent of such degrees in 1980, 36 percent in 1990, and 44 percent by 2000.[56]

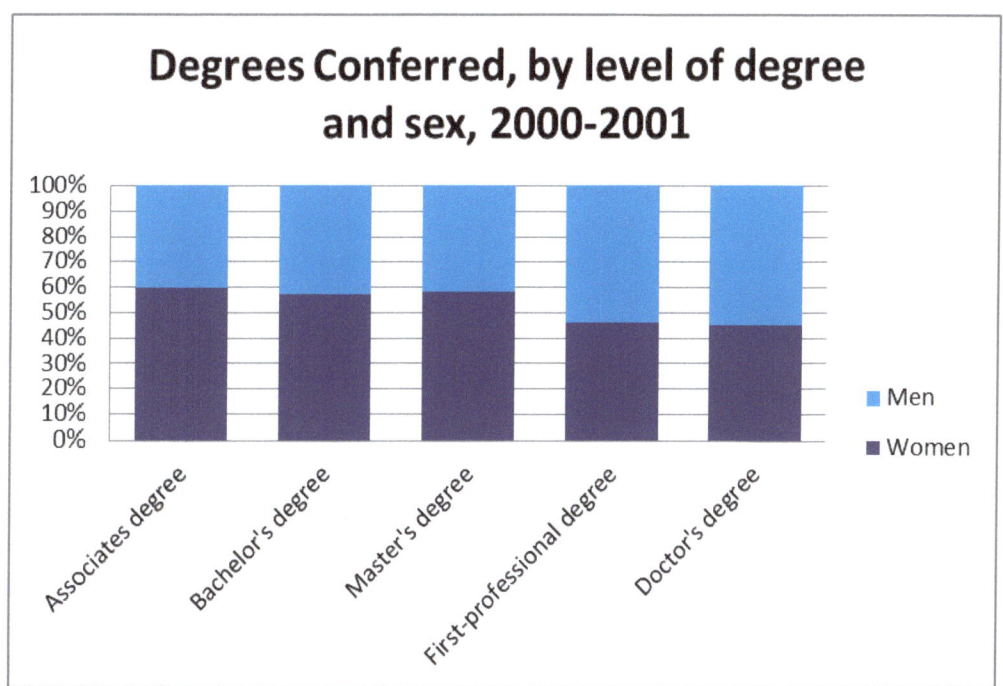

Source: Data from the National Center for Education Statistics, (2010) "Degrees Conferred by degree-granting institutions, by level of degree and sex of student: Selected years, 1869-70 through 2019-20."

Women who increased their educational attainment saw substantial gains in income but did not match the earnings of men with comparable education levels. By 1985, women with a Bachelor's Degree or higher witnessed their median weekly earnings match those of men holding just a high school diploma or equivalent. In 1992, these women's wages continued to climb until they bypassed the wages of men having received some college education or holding an associate's degree. These increases in wages continued through the remainder of the 1990s, but the wages of women with a Bachelor's Degree or higher remained lower than those of men with similar levels of education. Men with four years of college or more also saw real wage increases during this timeframe, so, in 2000, their earnings were approximately 35 percent higher than that of women with the same level of education.[57]

The increased educational attainment of women contributed greatly to their overall increased earnings from 1980 to 2000 – with women's usual median weekly earnings growing by 23.4 percent over this time period.[58] However, most of the gains in earning power were reserved for women with a Bachelor's Degree or higher. The pay for these women increased by approximately 31 percent from 1980 to 2000. In comparison, women with less education saw much smaller or even no changes in earnings. Pay for women with some college rose by approximately 9 percent, while the real earnings of women with a high school diploma were virtually unchanged and decreased for women having less than a high school diploma.[59]

Women's Labor Force Participation Rates Continue to Increase; Married Women Maintain Participation Rates through Prime Child Bearing and Child Rearing Years

Over the last two decades of the 20th Century, women of all races continued to participate in the labor force in increasing numbers – with gains especially noticeable among married women with children. In 1980, White women's labor force participation rates were close to that of Black women at 51.2 and 53.1 percent, respectively, while Hispanic women's labor force participation rate had climbed to 47.4 percent. Between 1990 and 2000, Black women took the lead again in labor force participation – with 58.3 percent in 1990 and 63.1 percent in 2000, compared to White women, whose participation rate was 57.4 percent in 1990 and 59.5 percent in 2000. Hispanic women's labor force participation rate also grew from 53.1 percent in 1990 to 57.5 percent by 2000. When labor force participation data for Asian women first was collected in 1990, it showed the same labor force participation rates between White and Asian women in 1990 and 2000.[60] Even more significant was the increase in the labor force participation rate of married mothers with children, which climbed from 54.1 percent in 1980 to 66.3 percent in 1990 and 70.6 percent in 2000.[61]

For women with young children, marital status remained a significant factor in labor force participation. In 1980, mothers with children had similar labor force participation rates whether they were single (52 percent) or married (54.1 percent), while women who were divorced, widowed or separated had a higher labor force participation rate of 69.4 percent. By 2000, all mothers had increased their participation rate. For those who were divorced, widowed or separated, it reached 82.7 percent, while the rate for single mothers rose to 73.9 percent, and married mothers had a slightly lower participation rate of 70.6 percent.[62] The trend toward women remaining attached to the labor force through their prime child bearing and child rearing years continued during the latter half of the 20th Century and began to follow the pattern of men's labor force participation. In 1980 and 1990, women's labor force participation rate by age peaked at ages 25-34, similar to the years that men's labor force participation rate was highest. However, by 2000, the peak years for labor force participation had edged up to the 35-44 year age brackets for both women and men.[63]

Contribution of Married Women's Income to Family Income Grows

The contribution of married women's earnings to overall family income also grew steadily during the latter half of the 20th Century – from just over a quarter of all family income (26.7 percent) in 1980 to one-third of family income (33.5 percent) in 2000.[64] In 1987, the Bureau of Labor Statistics began to collect data on the percentage of wives whose earnings were higher than their husband's, noting that, in 1987, 23.7 percent of wives earned more than their husbands, some of whom may not have worked at all. Among couples where both the husband and wife worked, 17.8 percent of wives earned the higher wages. This trend grew steadily throughout the 1990s, and by 2000, 29.9 percent of wives had higher earnings in families where the husband may not have been working. In families where both spouses worked, 23.3 percent of wives earned higher wages than their husbands.[65]

Women's increased education and movement into higher-paying jobs may be one factor that accounts for the growth in families with higher-earning wives; however, another likely factor is the lack of increase in real earnings for men from 1980 to 2000. During this timeframe, women's real earnings rose by 23.4 percent on average, but men's earnings were essentially unchanged.[66] In its September 1997 report, *Money Income in the United States: 1996*, the U.S. Census Bureau noted that the narrowing of the wage gap was not necessarily cause for celebration. "Recent increases in the female-to-male earnings ratio have been due more to declines in the earnings of men than to increases in the earnings of women," it said.[67] By 2000, earnings for both men and women had started to rise slowly again; however, the wage gap held steady at 73.7 percent.[68]

Wage Gap Narrows Significantly in the 1980s, but Progress Slows During the 1990s

The last two decades of the 20th Century were marked by significant growth in the educational attainment of women, as well as a significant narrowing of the wage gap between women and men as women enjoyed the returns on their higher investments in education and accumulated labor-market experience. In 1980, the ratio between women's and men's earnings stood at 60.2 percent. Over these two decades, the wage gap narrowed considerably – the wage ratio reached 71.6 percent by 1990, and 73.7 percent by 2000.[69]

In 1998, the President's Council of Economic Advisors (CEA) issued a report which found that, although the pay gap had narrowed substantially between the signing of the Equal Pay Act in 1963 and 1998, "there still exists a significant wage gap that cannot be explained by differences between male and female workers in labor market experience and in the characteristics of jobs they hold." The report cited a detailed longitudinal study in the 1980s that found about one-third of the gender pay gap was explained by differences in the skills and experience that women bring to the labor market, and another 28 percent was due to differences in industry, occupation and union status among men and women. Roughly 40 percent of the pay gap could not be explained. The CEA concluded that "one indirect and rough measure of the extent of discrimination remaining in the labor market is the 'unexplained' difference in pay."[70]

Enforcement Actions

In the 1980s and 1990s, the EEOC enforcement activities included significant work on behalf of working women seeking equal opportunity and equal pay. In 1980, the EEOC held hearings on sex-based job segregation and wage discrimination; and, commissioned by the EEOC, the National Academy of Sciences published a report in 1981 entitled, *Women, Work and Wages: Equal Pay for Jobs of Equal Value.*

In 1984, General Motors Corporation (GM) and the United Auto Workers agreed to pay $42.4 million to resolve an EEOC Commissioner charge alleging the company engaged in a "pattern and practice" of race and sex discrimination. The settlement also provided that GM would promote a substantial number of minorities and women into managerial jobs, as well as recruit minorities and women into high-paying apprenticeship and craft programs. At that time, the settlement was the largest non-litigated settlement in the history of the EEOC.

One significant compensation case, *EEOC v. Allstate Insurance*, resulted in a 1985 consent decree between the EEOC and Allstate, resolving an Equal Pay Act claim that the company paid a lower guaranteed minimum salary to females than to males performing the identical job of sales agent. Under this decree, $5 million was distributed to approximately 3,200 women. In the same year, the Commission successfully settled a sex discrimination suit against Teachers Insurance and Annuity Equity Fund. This suit resulted in recalculating pension benefits in a "sex neutral manner" for over 800,000 female workers.

In 1986, the EEOC published its Interpretations of the Equal Pay Act, replacing those issued by the U.S. Department of Labor.

In 1995, the EEOC held a series of meetings devoted to hearing the views of experts and advocates on the effectiveness of the EEOC in its enforcement of laws prohibiting discrimination in employment. In his opening statement, EEOC Chairman Gilbert F. Casellas observed that "[t]he Commission has been criticized for paying insufficient attention to wage disparity" and stated that "[o]ur summons, with the help of the organizations present today, is to better use the tools provided by our existing authority to force employers who perpetuate wage-based inequities to examine their motivations and rectify the wrongs." In 1994, 9,600 charges of wage discrimination were filed with the Commission under the Equal Pay Act, Title VII of the Civil Rights Act, Title I of the Americans with Disabilities Act, and the Age Discrimination in Employment Act. Most of the charges were brought under Title VII, and the lion's share of the Title VII cases were based on race and/or gender.

In 1997, the EEOC issued an Enforcement Guidance on Sex Discrimination in the Compensation of Sports Coaches in Educational Institutions.[71] The Commission issued this guidance because, although Congress had outlawed sex-discrimination in school-sponsored athletics programs over twenty-five years prior (with the passage of Title IX), then-recent studies showed that the overall pattern of the employment and compensation of coaches by educational institutions was still far from gender-neutral. The Commission wanted to assist both coaches and educational institutions in better understanding their rights and responsibilities.

In addition to the EEOC's efforts, at the U.S. Department of Labor, the Office of Federal Contract Compliance Programs (OFCCP) initiated significant enforcement actions for continued wage discrimination by federal contractors under Executive Order 11246 (prohibiting federal government contractors from discriminating in employment on the basis of race, color, religion, national origin and, because of the later amendment, sex). The single largest financial recovery under Executive Order 11246 was obtained in 1989 against the Harris Trust and Savings Bank in Chicago, Illinois. This settlement brought to conclusion an 11-year race and sex discrimination case raising issues involving placement, pay, and promotion, with the bank agreeing to pay $14 million to women and minority group members who were employed between May 1973 and December 1988. In 1993, OFCCP began a practice of so-called "glass ceiling audits," specifically focusing on corporate management practices. The first settlement under this program was with Fairfax Hospital in Virginia, which provided over $600,000 in back pay and salary adjustments to 52 women. Through these specialized reviews and other regular compliance evaluations and complaint investigations, OFCCP investigators found and remedied other instances of pay discrimination. For example, in 1999, after concluding that Texaco Corporation underpaid 186 female workers, OFCCP recovered a total of $3.1 million in back pay and salary increases on their behalf. That same year, OFCCP reached a settlement for $4.5 million with the Boeing Company in a sex and pay discrimination case. Boeing also agreed to redesign its tracking process for hiring and promotions.

Military Conflict	Number of Women Served
Spanish-America War	1,500
WW1	10,000+
WW2	40,000
Korean War	120,000
Vietnam Era	7,000
Persian Gulf War	41,000
OEF / OIF	200,000+

Source: U.S. Department of Veterans Affairs. America's Women Veterans: Military Service History and VA Benefit Utilization Services (2011),http://www.va.gov/vetdata/docs/SpecialReports/Final_Womens_Report_3_2_12_v_7.pdf

2000-2010: Progress Stalls, Enforcement Efforts Redoubled

An Overview of the Economic Climate

The 21st Century unfolded with great hope and expectations. As technology transformed our basic means of communication and revolutionized our workplaces, it carried a promise for easing the work-life challenge experienced by the majority of working families, opening more opportunities for women in the growing technology sector and continued progress in closing the wage gap between women and men.[72] Yet, despite these hopes, the early years of the 21st Century are notable for stalled progress and dips in labor force participation, particularly among working mothers of young children.

A volatile first decade of the 21st Century brought the worst economic crisis since the Great Depression, which greatly changed the economic conditions of our nation and increased the economic pressure felt by families all across the country. The heightened need for security and build-up of military units also brought with it more opportunities for women to serve in the ultimate non-traditional jobs – military occupational specialties in the U.S. armed forces. The number of women in the military has varied greatly over the years, but reached a high of over 200,000 women during the Operation Enduring Freedom and Operation Iraqi Freedom (OEF/OIF) conflicts.[73]

While women's contributions to family income rose in importance in the lead-up to 2000, the new century's economic challenges illustrated that women's earnings often proved crucial to families' financial survival.

Increased Educational Attainment and its Effect on Earnings

The new century began with women holding solid majorities in the attainment of Bachelor's, Master's and Doctoral Degrees, earning 57 percent of all Bachelor's Degrees and 58.5 percent of all Master's Degrees in 2000. These numbers held steady for Bachelor's Degrees through 2009 but increased slightly for post-graduate degrees, with women awarded 60.4 percent of all Master's Degrees, 49 percent of all first professional degrees, and 52.3 percent of Doctoral Degrees by the end of the decade.[74]

Education continued to be an important factor in increasing women's earnings throughout the first part of the 21st Century, but the earnings gains were not shared equally by women of different races/ethnicities. In 2011, among women of all race/ethnic groups with Bachelor's Degrees, Asian women had the highest median weekly earnings, at $946. White women followed with median weekly earnings of $939, while Hispanic women and Black women had significantly lower median weekly earnings – $862 and $843, respectively.[75]

From 2000 to 2010, real median earnings for full-time, year-round male workers remained mostly unchanged, while women's earnings edged up by 3.4 percent early in the decade, then held steady through 2011.[76] Educational attainment was an important factor in earnings, even though a wage gap between educated women and men persisted. College-educated workers saw the highest financial returns to their education. Meanwhile, men without advanced education saw earnings drop, and women with lower educational attainment saw little movement in wages.[77] These trends influenced the slight change in the female-to-male wage ratio, which rose from 73.7 percent to 76.3 percent between 2000 and 2001. The wage ratio has hovered near this point throughout the remainder of the 2000s – hitting a high of 77.8 percent in 2007, only to retreat to 77 percent in 2011.[78]

Changes in Labor Force Participation Rates

Between 2000 and 2010, labor force participation rates declined slightly for all women, but most dramatically for Black women, going from a high of 63.1 percent in 2000 to 59.9 percent by 2010. Black women still maintained higher labor force participation rates than other women, who saw only slight declines in their participation rates. In 2010, White women's labor force participation rate was 58.5 percent, Hispanic women's rate stood at 56.5 percent, and Asian women were at 57.0 percent.[79] During this time period, the labor force participation rates of men also dropped, reflecting the impact of the recession, as well as an increase in the number of older workers retiring from the labor force.

The labor force participation rate of married mothers, with spouse present, also declined during this period, dropping from 70.6 percent in 2000[80] to 69.7 percent in 2010.[81] For women with young children, being married was associated with a lower labor force participation rate. In 2010, mothers with children under age 6 who were married, with spouse present, had a labor force participation rate of 62.5

percent, while mothers with all other marital statuses had a rate of 68.2 percent.[82] The drop in married mothers' labor force participation rate, particularly the rate for those with young children, led to considerable public discussion about the difficulties that professional women with children faced in the workforce.

The older workers' role in the economy also took on greater significance during the early 2000s. Women's labor force participation rates by age continued to follow the trends for men through the early part of the 21st Century, with both men and women having the highest labor force participation rates later in life – in the 45-54 year-old age bracket. This shift in the ages of peak labor force participation, with a higher participation rate among the 45-54 year olds, is markedly different from the previous fifty years and is one reflection of the greater presence of older workers in the labor force as the U.S. population ages.[83]

Contribution of Married Women's Income to Family Income

The contribution of married women's earnings to overall family income continued to grow steadily throughout the first decade of the 21st Century, going from 33.5 percent in 2000 to 37.6 percent by 2010.[84] The percentage of wives with higher incomes than their husbands grew even more dramatically. In 2000, 29.9 percent of wives earned more than their husbands, some of whom may not have worked at all, and by 2010, this figure had reached 38.8 percent. Among couples where both the husband and wife worked, 23.3 percent of wives had higher earnings than their husbands in 2000, while 29.2 percent of wives were the higher earner by 2010.[85]

Source: U.S. Census Bureau. (2011). "Women's Earnings as a Percentage of Men's Earnings by Race and Hispanic Origin." *Historical Income Tables.* http://www.census.gov/hhes/www/income/data/historical/people/.

Enforcement Actions

From fiscal year 2000 to 2009, the EEOC found reasonable cause to believe discrimination had occurred in 829 charges of pay discrimination under all of the statutes it enforces, and recovered over $52.7 million for charging parties in those cases through administrative enforcement.[86] The EEOC also litigated a significant number of sex-based wage discrimination cases throughout this decade, including the 2004 case *EEOC v. Morgan Stanley & Co.*, in which the EEOC obtained $54 million for sex-based discrimination in compensation, promotion, and other aspects of employment.

With more women serving as the primary or co-breadwinner in families, concern increased about long working hours and the conflict experienced by women and men who were both in the workforce and responsible for caring for young children, elderly parents or disabled family members.[87] The EEOC sought to address this issue in 2007 with enforcement guidance on unlawful disparate treatment of workers with caregiving responsibilities.[88]

In 2007, the Supreme Court issued its ruling in *Ledbetter v. Goodyear Tire & Rubber Co.*,[89] igniting controversy when it struck down the longstanding interpretation of Title VII's timeliness rules held by the EEOC and many courts. The case began in March 1998, when Lilly Ledbetter, who was employed at the Gadsden, Alabama, plant of Goodyear Tire and Rubber Company, filed a charge with the EEOC alleging that she had received a discriminatorily low salary as an area manager because of her sex in violation of Title VII of the Civil Rights Act. Ledbetter only discovered how much her male co-workers were making when someone left an anonymous note in her mailbox showing her pay and that of the three males who were doing the same job. In an interview, she stated that she worked for a company that told her, "You do not discuss wages with anyone in this factory."[90] The court ruled that, because the later effects of past discrimination did not restart the clock for filing an EEOC charge, Ledbetter's claim was untimely. The outcome was at odds with the longstanding interpretation of wage discrimination timeliness rules held by the EEOC and many courts, and highlighted the significant problem of pay secrecy.

The Ledbetter case helped raise the visibility of the equal pay issue and generated a major organizing campaign to reverse the decision in Congress. In response, Congress passed and President Obama signed the Lilly Ledbetter Fair Pay Act of 2009, effectively restoring the previous timelines for filing Title VII charges of pay discrimination with the EEOC. Further, President Obama addressed the ongoing challenge of equal pay and the persistent wage gap between women and men by creating the National Equal Pay Task Force in January 2010.[91]

During this decade, OFCCP continued to address pay discrimination through its enforcement activity under Executive Order 11246. In 2002, a $4.1 million settlement with Coca Cola for pay discrimination on the basis of race and sex benefitted over 900 current and former female employees at the company's Atlanta, Georgia, headquarters, many of whom held professional positions. In 2004, OFCCP resolved another large systemic pay discrimination case combining the issues of pay and sex discrimination in a $5.5 million settlement with Charlotte, North Carolina-based Wachovia Corporation. In that case, OFCCP alleged that more than 2,000 female workers had been underpaid.

II. 2010 and Beyond: Working to Close the Gap

We have witnessed five decades of economic progress for women, supported by the expansion of civil rights and sweeping changes in the role of women in the workplace and our national economy. Yet women still face a significant gender gap in pay, one that seems to be closing far more slowly than in earlier decades, despite significant gains in education and workforce participation.

There are multiple ways to measure the pay gap – but under all of them, and with or without considering occupation, female and minority workers earn significantly less than White male workers. According to the latest Bureau of Labor Statistics data, women's weekly median earnings are about 81 percent of men's.[92] And looking at annual earnings reveals even larger gaps – approximately 23 cents less on the dollar for women compared with men.[93] The wage gap also is greater for women of color: Black women earn approximately 70 cents and Hispanic women make approximately 60 cents for every dollar earned by a non-Hispanic White man, according to Bureau of Labor Statistics data; and 64 cents for Black women and 56 cents for Hispanic women, according to Census data. Minority men face a wage gap as well when compared to White men – about 21 cents for Black men and about 29 cents for Hispanic men based on weekly wage data.[94] Ultimately, no matter how you look at the data, a persistent pay gap remains. Decades of research shows a gender gap in pay even after factors such as the type of work performed and qualifications (education and experience) are taken into account. These studies consistently conclude that discrimination likely explains at least some of the remaining difference. [95]

Fifty years later, we still have much work to do. We can continue to improve existing federal enforcement efforts through better strategic collaboration, and improve data collection and investigative tools. We can pass the Paycheck Fairness Act, so the Equal Pay Act will better safeguard the right to equal pay for equal work. Finally, we can expand our vision of equal opportunity. We can take on the array of practices and preconceptions – such as occupational segregation – that contribute to inequality for working women (and some men). We can break down the remaining barriers that prevent us from achieving true equality in the workplace.

Closing the pay gap is not just a moral imperative; it would confer broad economic and social benefits on our nation, its workers, and their families. Ensuring that workers who are underpaid due to discrimination can earn a fair wage means they can better support themselves and their families, thereby lifting countless children out of poverty. It also will help grow the middle class. Over the long-term, equal pay will provide a broader economic base for our nation – one that benefits all workers and their families.

A. 50 Years Later – Not Equal, Not Yet

Today, the U.S. workforce is rich in diversity of gender, race and age. Overall, 58.1 percent of U.S. women were in the labor force in 2011, with Black women continuing to lead at 59.1 percent and White women close behind at 58 percent. Asian women's participation in the labor force stood at 56.8, and Hispanic women had the lowest rate at 55.9 percent.[96] Working mothers continue to represent a significant number of working women, and their labor force participation rates were highest for single mothers at 74.9 percent, while married women had a rate of 69.1 percent. A majority of older women, 59.5 percent of those aged 54 to 65, were present in the workforce. These figures are just slightly lower than the historic labor force participation rates that were achieved in 1999, and show that a majority of women remain strongly attached to paid employment.[97]

Women continue to lead in educational attainment, earning more Bachelor's, Master's and Doctoral Degrees than men and nearly half of all professional degrees. Women's choice of college major also holds promise for greater gains in non-traditional occupations. Recent female college graduates are now earning nearly half of all the degrees in natural resources and conservation, homeland security and law enforcement, half of all business administration degrees, and more than half of all degrees in biological sciences and the health professions.[98]

And in the field of entrepreneurship, women's growing presence represents a total economic impact of nearly $3 trillion to the U.S. economy. In 2008, women entrepreneurs produced employment for over 23 million workers – especially significant considering that only 20 percent of women-owned firms had employees.

Despite these gains, the workforce continues to be segregated by race and gender – particularly when it comes to occupation. This occupational segregation has important implications for closing the pay gap, because women are segregated into low-paying occupations and also typically earn less than men in the same field. Addressing the barriers that prevent women from having equal access to higher-paying occupations and ensuring fair pay within occupations are critical strategies for closing the pay gap.

In addition to gender differences in occupations, there are differences based on race and ethnicity. For example, White and Asian women are more likely to work in higher-paying management, professional and related occupations than Black and Hispanic women, who are more likely to work in lower-paying service occupations and significantly more likely to be among the working poor.[99]

Occupational segregation has decreased since the mid-20th Century but is far from elimination.[100] Forty-four percent of employed men work in occupations that are over three-quarters male, while only 6 percent of working women are in these same occupations.[101] As recently as 2010, nine of the ten most common occupations for women were majority female – administrative assistants, nurses, cashiers, retail salespersons, nursing and home health aides, waitresses, retail sales supervisors and managers, customer service representatives, and house cleaners.[102] Examples of fields that remain at least 75 percent male include manufacturing salespersons, farmers and ranchers, architects, transportation supervisors, cutting workers, detectives and investigators, and computer programmers.[103]

Occupational segregation has persisted despite the many other economic and social transformations described in Part I of this report. Indeed, the top 10 occupations held by women did not vary much between 1960 and 1980. Nursing aides, orderlies and attendants appeared among the top 10 list for the first time in 1975, but remained among top jobs for women until 2000.[104] In 2010, the list looked little different than in 1980 – with variation in the leading occupations often due to changes in definitions and occupational groupings over time.

Ten Leading Occupations of Women in Rank Order by Numbers of Women, 1960, 1980, 2000 and 2010				
Occupations	**1960**	**1980**	**2000**	**2010**
Private household workers	1	8	---	
Secretaries*(1)	2	1	1	
Retail trade, sales clerks*(2)	3	3		
Elementary school teachers*(3)	4	7	4	
Bookkeepers*(4)	5	2		
Waiters and waitresses	6	5		7
Nurses, professional (Registered Nurses)	7	6	6	2
Sewers and stichers, manufacturing	8	---		
Typists	9	9	---	
Cashiers	10	4	8	4
Nursing aides, orderlies, & attendants*(5)	---	10	7	
Retail & personal sales workers, including cashiers*(2)			2	
Managers & administrators, n.e.c.			3	
Sales supervisors & proprietors			5	
Bookkeepers, accounting, & auditing clerks*(4)			9	
Accountants & auditors			10	
Secretaries & administrative assistants* (1)				1
Elementary & middle school teachers *(3)				3
Cashiers				4
Retail salespersons *(2)				5
Nursing, psychiatric, and home health aides *(5)				6
First-line supervisors/managers of retail sales workers				8
Customer service representatives				9
Maids & housekeeping cleaners				10

Sources: Census Bureau. *U.S. Census Population: 1960*, Vol. 1; *Statistical Abstract of the United States: 1963;* and U.S. Bureau of Labor Statistics, *Labor Force Statistics Derived from the Current Population Survey: A Databook, Vol. 1 (1982),* and U.S. Department of Labor Women's Bureau, *"Leading Occupations for Women in 2000",* and *"20 Leading Occupations of Employed Women, 2010 Annual Averages" (based on BLS Current Population Survey data).*

Notes: *() notes a change in the name and or occupational grouping with a number that corresponds to a closely related occupation

In 1960, among non-traditional occupations for women – those in which women constituted 25 percent or less of those employed – women mostly held jobs on farms, in offices and retail establishments, or as clerks and sales positions for manufacturers, real estate or postal offices. Over the next twenty years, many of these occupations began to employ even greater numbers of women, so they no longer were male-dominated occupations. For instance, buyers in department stores, real estate agents, sales representatives and clerks in manufacturing facilities, managers in food and dairy stores, accountants and auditors and postal clerks all moved off the list of jobs that were non-traditional for women. Indeed, the decline in occupational segregation between 1970 and 2009 was largely a result of women moving into traditionally-male, white-collar occupations;[105] as a result, heavily male jobs have become increasingly blue-collar.

In recent decades, two areas that historically were almost exclusively male – the STEM fields and the military – have begun to open to women. By 1980, thanks to advances in women's educational attainment, the number of women in STEM fields began to increase – even though women still comprised 25 percent or less of the total employed in the STEM occupations. Notably, women who hold STEM degrees and work in STEM occupations earn 33 percent more, on average, than women in non-STEM jobs; and, while women in non-STEM occupations typically earn 23 percent less than their male colleagues, the salaries of their counterparts in STEM fields are only 14 percent less than those of their male co-workers.[106]

Women's service in the active duty armed forces steadily increased, especially after 2000. A total of 41,000 women served in the military during the Persian Gulf War.[107] By the end of November 2012, the number of women in the military reached 204,973. Of that total, 38,378 women were officers, and 164,021 women were enlisted.[108]

In recent years, changes in both law and policy have altered women's roles and the military jobs they are allowed to perform. Throughout U.S. military history, various rules and regulations have limited women's official involvement, rank attainment, and role within the services. However, according to the Pentagon, women frequently found themselves in combat during the wars in Iraq and Afghanistan. Hundreds of thousands of women have deployed in those conflicts and, unlike in previous wars, performed numerous functions that effectively put them directly in harm's way.[109] In January 2013, then-Secretary Leon Panetta recognized the exceptional service of women in the Iraq and Afghanistan wars by moving to open more military positions – including positions in ground combat – to women.

While occupational segregation is sometimes described as a simple matter of women's choices, historical patterns of exclusion and discrimination paint a more complex picture. Two general frameworks can explain occupational segregation: one based on workers and one based on employers. On the employer side, occupational segregation may be due to discrimination that can take several forms, including outright refusal to hire, severe harassment of women in non-traditional jobs, or policies and practices that screen qualified women out of positions but are not job-related.[110] An alternative framework emphasizes worker differences. For example, one group may be more willing to accept unpleasant or dangerous work, longer hours, or physical strain in return for higher wages. As another example, women may enter occupations that require less investment and result in less earnings growth because they expect abbreviated and discontinuous labor force activity.[111]

These two frameworks are not incompatible: the interaction between labor market discrimination and societal discrimination may have indirect effects that reinforce gender differences. For example, labor market discrimination can affect women's economic status indirectly by reducing their incentives to invest in themselves and to acquire particular job qualifications.[112]

For example, women are significantly underrepresented in STEM fields. According to statistics available from the National Center for Education Statistics, in 1970, fewer than 10 percent of new Bachelor's Degree graduates in business, computer science, engineering and newly graduating doctors and lawyers were women. By 2010, women were equally likely to graduate in business, law, and medicine as men.

However, less than one-third of new computer science graduates, and an even smaller fraction of new engineers, were women. A survey of undergraduate women at the University of Minnesota found that female undergraduates expressed lack of interest, had expectations of not being welcome in the profession, as well as exaggerated impressions of difficulty of the coursework in these fields.[113] Another study found that women were more likely to leave engineering compared to other fields because of dissatisfaction over pay and promotion opportunities.[114]

Regardless of the underlying causes, occupational segregation fuels the wage gap because average wages in "female" occupations are lower, even holding constant other observable characteristics such as education. This pattern is illustrated in Table 1, which highlights the most segregated occupations for each type of degree required. As the table shows, average wages in typically "female" occupations are significantly lower for each degree requirement category.

Table 1: Average Wages for Male and Female Dominated Professions

Male Dominated Professions Requiring a High School Diploma	Percent Male	Average Wage	Female Dominated Professions Requiring a High School Diploma	Percent Female	Average Wage
Brickmasons, blockmasons, and stonemasons	99 9	$ 45,410	Secretaries and administrative assistants	95.3	$ 34,660
Tool and die makers	99 2	$ 39,910	Childcare workers	94.1	$ 19,300
Pipelayers, plumbers, pipefitters, and steamfitters	98.7	$ 46,660	Hairdressers, hairstylists, and cosmetologists	92.8	$ 22,500
Carpenters	98.4	$ 39,530	Receptionists and information clerks	91.5	$ 25,240
Electricians	98 2	$ 48,250	Tellers	87.3	$ 24,100
Average		**$ 43,952**	**Average**		**$ 25,160**
Male Dominated Professions Requiring a Bachelor's Degree or Higher	Percent Male	Average Wage	Female Dominated Professions Requiring a Bachelor's Degree or Higher	Percent Female	Average Wage
Mechanical engineers	95 5	$ 78,160	Speech-language Pathologists	95.2	$ 66,920
Computer control programmers and operators	91.6	$ 71,380	Occupational Therapists	94	$ 72,320
Aerospace engineers	91	$ 97,480	Dietitians and nutritionists	93.3	$ 53,250
Electrical and electronics engineers	91	$ 87,180	Librarians	86.8	$ 54,500
Chiroprators	88.7	$ 67,200	Special education teachers	86.2	$ 53,220
Average		**$ 80,280**	**Average**		**$ 60,042**

Note: Occupations grouped by entry-level education requirement reported in the BLS Occupational Outlook Handbook.

Source: Bureau of Labor Statistics, Current Population Survey, Occupational Outlook Handbook.

To see the extent to which occupational segregation affects average wages, we plot the relationship between the average wage in the occupation—relative to what would be expected given the age and education level of the workers in the occupation—and the share of females in the occupation.[115] Figure 1 shows these results. Each observation corresponds to an occupation. There is a distinct negative relationship between average wage in the occupation and female share, with every 10 percentage point increase in female share associated with a 4 percent decline in average wages. In other words, women in female-dominated occupations seem to earn less than we would otherwise expect based on their age and education. And while we do not know the extent to which this phenomenon is explained by historical patterns of exclusion and present-day discrimination, or by worker decisions, or by a combination of the two, decreasing the degree of occupational segregation could have a significant impact on closing the wage gap.

Figure 1: Occupation Specific Wage and Female Share

Log Wage in Occupation Relative to Average Log

Coef: -0.0035
Std Err: 0.0003

Share Female

Note: The vertical axis corresponds to the occupation average wages that would be expected given the age and education level of workers
Source: March Current Population Survey, 2010 - 2012

In addition to the effects of occupational segregation, research findings and Bureau of Labor Statistics data show women regularly are paid less than men working in the same occupation and in some cases even the same job. Controlling for differences in the types of jobs women and men typically perform, women earn less than men in male-dominated occupations (such as managers, software developers, and CEOs) and in female-dominated occupations (such as teachers, nurses, and receptionists).[116] The pay gap exists for women with advanced degrees, corporate positions, and high-paying and high-skill jobs, just as it does for low- and middle-income workers. For example, in a recent study of newly trained doctors, even after controlling for the effects of specialty, practice setting, work hours and other factors, the gender pay gap was nearly $17,000 in 2008.[117]

A widely debated contention about the pay gap is that it is attributable to women's choices to put family ahead of work. However, the gender pay gap exists for women working full time as well as part time, and begins when women are first employed, which is often well before they have children.[118] Regardless of whether work hours could explain some portion of the wage gap, research shows there is a "motherhood penalty" for female workers with children, stemming from stereotypes and biases about working mothers. Researchers have found the mere fact of parenthood for women leads to perceptions of lowered competence and commitment, and lower salary offers.[119] The same research shows, however, that men are not penalized for having children and in some ways benefit.

To the extent discrimination limits the opportunities for women to enter more highly paid occupations, we need strategies designed to open these doors. To the extent that equal pay for equal work remains elusive, we must redouble our efforts. Understanding the impact of family responsibilities on the pay gap and ensuring that women are not penalized for their status as mothers is another important part of closing the gap over the long term. The next section sheds light on those strategies – including enforcement, education, training, and more tools for workers to know their worth and how to act on it.

B. Closing the Gap – The Way Forward

On January 27, 2010, during his State of the Union address, President Obama pledged "to crack down on violations of equal pay laws – so that women get equal pay for an equal day's work."[120] To carry out that pledge to strengthen federal equal pay enforcement, the White House simultaneously announced the creation of a National Equal Pay Task Force composed of the major federal agencies that enforce our nation's pay discrimination laws. The Task Force brings together the expertise and resources of four federal agencies: the Equal Employment Opportunity Commission (EEOC), the Department of Justice (DOJ), the Department of Labor (DOL), and the Office of Personnel Management (OPM). Collectively, these agencies have jurisdiction over several key federal employment laws that protect our nation's public and private sector workers.[121] Both the achievements of the Task Force and its member agencies and its agenda for the coming years help frame a national strategy to close the pay gap once and for all.

As the White House announcement explained:

> The President is establishing a National Equal Pay Task Force. To make sure we uphold our nation's core commitment to equality of opportunity, the Obama Administration is implementing an Equal Pay initiative to improve compliance, public education, and enforcement of equal pay laws. The Task Force will ensure that the agencies with responsibility for equal pay enforcement are coordinating efforts and limiting potential gaps in enforcement. The Administration also continues to support the Paycheck Fairness Act, and is increasing funding for the agencies enforcing equal pay laws and other key civil rights statutes.[122]

The Task Force approach also reflected the larger goal of developing a unified civil rights agenda in the federal government. Just as intelligence agencies must share information to protect our national security, so too must civil rights agencies work together to safeguard the rights and economic security of all workers.

C. Achievements of the National Equal Pay Task Force

Shortly after the Task Force's creation, members developed a set of recommendations and goals to structure its collaboration on compliance, public education, and enforcement.[123] Those recommendations addressed five identified "persistent challenges" to the effective enforcement of equal pay laws, providing a road map for the work of the Task Force member agencies over the coming years:

1. Interagency Coordination. Different federal agencies have different federal responsibilities for equal pay enforcement under different laws, and lack of coordination leaves gaps in enforcement. The Task Force proposed to close those gaps and maximize the impact of existing enforcement tools through strengthened interagency coordination.

2. Available Data Sources. Existing available data sources on the private workforce are inadequate. The Task Force recommended improvements in data collection on the private workforce to better understand the pay gap and better apply limited enforcement resources.

3. Outreach and Public Education. Both employees and employers lack information about the wage gap and their legal rights and responsibilities. In response, the Task Force planned

extensive outreach and public education materials for employers and employees, as well as training programs for the investigators at their member agencies.

4. <u>Pay Gap in Federal Workforce.</u> An eleven-cent wage gap for the federal workforce shows the need to address these issues for public employees. The Task Force directed the EEOC and OPM to develop a plan to identify the sources of this gap and address them.

5. <u>Passage of the Paycheck Fairness Act.</u> Current laws addressing unequal pay could be strengthened through additional legislation. The Task Force supported passage of the Paycheck Fairness Act to address loopholes in current law.

> *In June 2011, OFCCP settled a lawsuit against multi-national pharmaceutical corporation AstraZeneca, involving claims the company paid certain female sales associates less than their male counterparts. Under the terms of the settlement, AstraZeneca agreed to pay $250,000 to 124 female employees who worked at the company's business center in Wayne, Pennsylvania. AstraZeneca also agreed to re-examine its pay practices in offices across 13 states and the District of Columbia, to determine if women in that position were being underpaid and to adjust salaries accordingly.*

In July 2010, Vice President Biden publicly released the Task Force recommendations.[124] Since then, Task Force member agencies have been building the infrastructure for an unprecedented level of collaboration across the federal government. By putting aside old turf battles and seeking opportunities to reduce duplication and maximize efficiency, Task Force members have been working to ensure that all workers get fair pay.

D. 2011 – 2013: Establishing the Infrastructure for Improved Equal Pay Enforcement

The early years of the Equal Pay Task Force's work largely consisted of developing the infrastructure for improved enforcement of equal pay laws, including achieving a number of specific milestones related to implementing the first recommendation of improved interagency coordination. This infrastructure development rested on two pillars: the development of mechanisms for interagency collaboration to enhance federal law enforcement agencies' capacity to identify and remedy illegal pay discrimination, and efforts to ensure federal regulations and policy provided the strongest possible framework for the enforcement of equal pay laws.

The development of mechanisms for improved interagency collaboration on equal pay laws also fostered a more integrated federal approach to civil rights enforcement broadly. Under the leadership of EEOC Chair Jacqueline Berrien, Assistant Attorney General for Civil Rights Tom Perez and OFCCP Director Patricia Shiu, agencies reinvigorated existing Memoranda of Understanding to facilitate information sharing, conducted pilot projects aimed at improving interagency collaboration in enforcement, built interagency relationships, facilitated joint outreach efforts, and trained together to ensure a shared understanding of civil rights laws and of each agency's role in enforcing them.

In November 2011, the EEOC and OFCCP issued a revised Memorandum of Understanding (MOU) aimed at strengthening collaboration between the two agencies. The revised MOU promotes effective collaboration in the agencies' enforcement efforts, reduces duplication, and maximizes efficiency. The EEOC and OFCCP conducted a pilot project in 2011 and 2012, focused on improving collaboration in enforcement, facilitating joint outreach, and maximizing efficiencies through joint training and cross training. Drawing on the improved information sharing provisions in the revised MOU, the EEOC and

OFCCP worked collaboratively on dozens of investigations and audits, conducted dozens of joint outreach events, and trained together on areas of shared jurisdiction, such as compensation discrimination. The collaboration conserved valuable tax dollars by avoiding duplicative effort, and helped lay the groundwork for interagency collaboration on more complex issues in the future.

The EEOC and DOJ also worked to improve interagency collaboration in the enforcement of federal civil rights laws, including equal pay laws. Through a pilot project involving the EEOC's Philadelphia, Chicago, Los Angeles and San Francisco District Offices, the EEOC and DOJ worked to improve collaboration early in EEOC's investigations of charges of discrimination against state and local government employers, thereby reducing the need for time-consuming and duplicative supplemental investigations. Since 2010, the EEOC and DOJ have collaborated on over 220 charges, on issues including pay discrimination and sex segregation in assignment. To date, lawsuits filed as a result of the project have included one involving sex-segregated job assignments at a correctional facility in Ohio and one involving the termination of an employee after she announced her pregnancy. Additionally, since the Task Force began, the EEOC and DOJ worked together to bring a joint enforcement action against the Texas Department of Agriculture in which the agencies obtained monetary relief under the Equal Pay Act and Title VII for three women who were paid less than their male counterparts.

Tabatha Wagner learned that she was paid less than a male colleague who was hired after her at Hyundai Ideal Electric Company. After she raised the issue, she was fired in retaliation for complaining. The EEOC sued, and in May 2011, Hyundai Ideal Electric agreed to pay $188,000 to Ms. Wagner to settle the lawsuit. As part of the settlement, the company also agreed to provide training for all human resource personnel and employees at their Mansfield, Ohio facility, to help prevent future violation of federal employment discrimination laws.

In addition to developing the infrastructure to support a robust interagency approach to equal pay enforcement, Task Force agencies spent considerable resources developing the strongest possible regulatory and policy framework to support it. One of the most notable achievements in this area was the rescission of two 2006 guidance documents known as the "Compensation Standards" and "Voluntary Guidelines" that created arbitrary barriers to OFCCP enforcement of pay discrimination in violation of Executive Order 11246. In addition to rescinding the old guidance documents, OFCCP provided new guidance for contractors and other interested stakeholders setting forth the procedures, analysis and protocols OFCCP will utilize going forward. These new procedures align OFCCP enforcement with Title VII principles, and with the approach of its sister agencies on the Task Force, the EEOC and DOJ.[125]

Since 2010, the Task Force also has been working to implement the second recommendation on improved data collection. In August 2010, the EEOC commissioned a study by the National Academy of Sciences to determine the type of pay data the EEOC should collect to enhance wage discrimination law enforcement, and how best to collect that data.[126] The National Academy of Sciences issued its report in August 2012, calling on the EEOC, DOJ and OFCCP to develop a comprehensive plan for the use of compensation data, and providing analysis of how compensation data may be used in enforcement efforts.[127] In August 2011, OFCCP issued an Advance Notice of Proposed Rulemaking (ANPRM) soliciting stakeholder input on the design and use of a potential compensation data collection tool.[128] The EEOC, OFCCP and DOJ are working in close coordination to develop integrated, complementary plans for pay data collection.

Task Force member agencies also have made progress on the third recommendation, better education and outreach for employees and employers. In collaboration with other National Equal Pay Act Task Force members, both the EEOC and the Women's Bureau initiated education and outreach events in cities across the nation to educate women about their rights and employers about their responsibilities. The Bureau released two new publications, *A Woman's Guide to Equal Pay Rights* and *An Employer's Guide to Equal Pay*, and an Equal Pay Toolkit, which can be found on the agency's website.[129] Led by the Women's Bureau, the Department of Labor, in conjunction with the Equal Pay Task Force, issued an "Equal Pay App Challenge." This challenge invited developers to use publicly available data and resources to create applications that accomplish at least one of the following goals: provide greater access to pay data broken down by gender, race, and ethnicity; provide interactive tools for early career coaching; help inform negotiations; or promote online mentoring. The winning apps, which help empower and educate users, were announced at a ceremony at the Department of Labor during the summer of 2012.[130]

All agencies also are collaborating on outreach and on training within their agencies, which saves resources and ensures a consistent federal strategy on equal pay. Some highlights include:

- The Department of Labor's Women's Bureau, in partnership with the Department's Office of Public Engagement and Center for Faith-Based Neighborhood Partnerships, convened a series of briefings to highlight the plight of America's most vulnerable workers. The series, named "Vulnerable Women Workers," assembled national women's organizations, private foundations and government agencies to learn more about the working conditions and gender-based pay equity challenges of vulnerable workers.

- In 2011, the EEOC hosted twenty-eight Equal Pay Day events around the country with participation from Task Force agency members, experts in equal pay advocacy, and private sector leaders. Over 2,000 people attended the various events, in cities such as Atlanta, Birmingham, Boston, New York, Phoenix, Miami, Nashville, Cheyenne, Los Angeles, and Salt Lake City.

- A 2012 Equal Pay Tweet Up, hosted by the Department of Labor with participants from the EEOC, DOJ and community leaders, was a nationally trending topic and generated substantial discussion and visibility around equal pay efforts.

- In 2013, the Women's Bureau co-led eighteen Equal Pay Day events around the country with participation from Task Force agency members, experts in equal pay advocacy, and private sector leaders. Over 1,100 people attended the various events, in cities such as Atlanta, Kansas City, Boston, Dallas, Denver, San Francisco, Seattle, Philadelphia, and Chicago.

- Also in 2013, in collaboration with the Department of Labor's OFCCP and Office of the Chief Economist, the Women's Bureau hosted an equal pay web chat. Experts from each of the agencies were on hand to discuss wage inequality and ongoing policy initiatives, and directed participants to resources designed to help workers. More than 350 people participated in the chat and received immediate responses to their many questions.

- Finally, the Women's Bureau maintains a webpage dedicated to providing the public with the most current tools, resources and information on equal pay. The page, found at http://www.dol.gov/equalpay/, includes the latest translations of guides for women and employers on equal pay rights and obligations, links to the facts sheets on women's earnings developed by the Women's Bureau and the Bureau of Labor Statistics, and OFCCP's Equal Pay Enforcement statistics.

The Task Force also is working to ensure the federal government is a model employer when it comes to ensuring equal pay for all workers, addressing the fourth recommendation outlined above. The EEOC and OPM continue to work closely on equal pay, building on the commitment made by EEOC Chair Jacqueline Berrien and then-OPM Director John Berry in their July 2011 joint memorandum to federal employees pledging their commitment to the vigorous enforcement of pay discrimination laws as they apply to federal employees. Task Force members, led by OPM, have developed a number of programs aimed at improving women's participation at the highest levels of federal service, including the development of an online portal for Federal Women Program Managers and programs on Work-Life Effectiveness.

> *Lorelei Kilker is an analytical chemist for an environmental laboratory. She lives in Brighton, Colorado with her domestic partner and their two children. In October 2011, Ms. Kilker was one of a class of women who benefitted from the EEOC's investigation of alleged systematic sex discrimination at her former employer. The EEOC found that Western Sugar denied women training and promotions, gave them less desirable work assignments and segregated positions by gender, denied year-round employment, and paid lower wages to women at its Ft. Morgan, Colorado facility.*
>
> *The EEOC obtained back wages and significant remedial relief through conciliation with the employer.*

In order to further understand how the practices of executive departments and agencies (agencies) affect the compensation of similarly situated men and women, and to promote gender pay equality in the federal government and more broadly, President Obama issued a May 10, 2013 Presidential Memorandum, titled "Advancing Pay Equality in the Federal Government and Learning from Successful Practices." The Presidential Memorandum directs OPM to submit a government-wide strategy to address any gender pay gap in the federal workforce. Each agency is required to review pay and promotion policies and practices to facilitate development of the strategy.

During this time, each agency also has substantially increased its effectiveness in the enforcement of pay discrimination laws, as a result of all of these specific improvements in collaboration, coordination, policy, outreach, training, and individual agency initiatives.

- From the Task Force's formation in January 2010 through March 31, 2013, the EEOC obtained over $78 million in relief for victims of sex-based wage discrimination through administrative enforcement.

- OFCCP similarly has recovered more than $33 million in back wages and nearly 7,000 job opportunities on behalf of over 60,000 victims of discrimination. During this period, OFCCP reviewed the pay practices of over 14,000 businesses that employ over 5.6 million workers – and closed more than 80 compliance evaluations with financial settlements remedying pay discrimination on the basis of gender and race. Through those efforts, OFCCP recovered a total of $2.5 million in back pay and salary adjustments for more than 1,200 workers who were victims of pay discrimination. In 2011, OFCCP more than doubled the number of compensation cases closed with financial remedies over the number closed in 2010 – and successfully resolved an even greater number of compensation cases in 2012.

- DOJ concentrated on opening opportunities for women in the higher paying law enforcement jobs and entered into settlements with police departments, correctional facilities, and other public employers where women are underrepresented in non-traditional positions.[131]

E. 2013 and Beyond: The Way Forward

As we mark the 50th Anniversary of the Equal Pay Act in 2013, the Task Force has achieved a number of the milestones that it set for itself in 2010 and is continuing to move forward, working toward passage of the Paycheck Fairness Act and addressing the broad array of issues that contribute to inequality for working women.

In 2013, Task Force agencies are moving from exploring collaboration and developing collaboration tools to making interagency collaboration a regular component of their agencies' enforcement work. This effort includes regular tri-agency meetings with the leadership of the EEOC, OFCCP and Department of Justice Civil Rights Division, active implementation of the revitalized MOU to ensure regular information-sharing between the EEOC and OFCCP at the headquarters level and among the agencies' field offices, and the application of the lessons of the interagency pilot projects to make specific improvements in enforcement procedures.

In addition, Task Force agencies are focusing on how better data can improve enforcement. One of the biggest obstacles to combating pay discrimination is that so many women do not know they are being underpaid due to discrimination and many employers prohibit the sharing of pay data. To address the implications of pay secrecy norms and policies, the Task Force continues to focus on the importance of pay data collection. The EEOC, OFCCP and DOJ continue to work closely together as they consider the use of pay data in enforcement efforts.

Better enforcement of existing civil rights laws will help, but those laws also leave gaps that must be filled. Congress, too, has an important role to play, by passing the Paycheck Fairness Act. This Act would address the current loopholes in existing law; strengthen remedies for pay discrimination; increase outreach and education to working women; provide technical assistance to small businesses; ensure that employees can discuss their wages without risk of being fired; and provide additional research and resources to fight pay inequity.

Finally, even with better enforcement and better laws, we also need an equal pay agenda that addresses the broad array of issues that contribute to wage inequality. We must continue to enforce the nation's laws prohibiting employers from paying women and men differently for the same work. And we also must address pay discrimination within a broader framework of practices that may limit the full economic participation of women workers.

Addressing Occupational Segregation

For example, we must break down discriminatory barriers that exclude women from traditionally male-dominated occupations, which pay more than traditionally female dominated occupations. In its work on sex discrimination issues, the DOJ has focused on cases that open non-traditional positions – such as police and correctional officer jobs – to women, and OFCCP has renewed its focus on increasing opportunities for women in the construction industry. OFCCP's new pay discrimination guidance also is intended to broaden the agency's focus on practices such as channeling and glass ceilings that wrongly exclude women from higher paying job opportunities. The EEOC always has been a leader in addressing systemic discrimination against women in employment through administrative enforcement and litigation efforts, and will continue to be a leader in this realm in the future. In sum, the agencies are working to ensure that these jobs – solid middle-class jobs that allow workers to provide for their families' futures – are not closed to women workers on the basis of sex.

For a number of years Amanda McMillan of Jackson, Mississippi worked as a secretary for the owner of a Forrest City Grocery Company. She was doing many of the same duties as male salespeople, but at lower pay. Despite repeatedly asking for a promotion to the better and higher-paying job in sales, she was told by the company that the job of a salesman was too dangerous for a woman, and that she would not be a good mother if she were on the road meeting customers.

The EEOC sued Forrest City for sex discrimination on McMillan's behalf, and obtained $125,000 in monetary damages and an agreement to provide ongoing training for management on sex discrimination.

When asked why she has pursued the case, McMillan said, "I'm doing this because it was wrong and I could never look my girls in the face and then tell them they live in America and could be anything they wanted to be."

In addition to improved enforcement, we can educate and empower workers to take better advantage of these open doors. One example is the focus that the Council on Women and Girls and White House Office of Science and Technology have placed on increasing the participation of women and girls, as well as other underrepresented groups, in the fields of science, technology, engineering, and mathematics. Strategies include increasing the engagement of girls with STEM subjects in formal and informal environments, encouraging mentoring to support women throughout their academic and professional experiences, and supporting efforts to retain women in the STEM workforce. Another example is providing workers better information, mentoring and negotiation tools, through apps such as those developed by the Department of Labor's app challenge.

Addressing the Overlay of Discrimination Based on Race, Ethnicity and Gender in Compensation

The pay gap for women of color compared with White men is bigger than the gap for all women compared with men. Task Force agencies enforce laws that challenge illegal pay discrimination whether it is based on race, national origin, disability, or gender, or a combination of factors. Understanding and addressing how the pay gap impacts women (and men) of color will be another important focus in 2013 and beyond.

Addressing Discrimination Against Mothers and Caregivers

Addressing the wage gap for women also includes addressing the problem of discrimination based on stereotypes about the proper role of women and mothers. Pregnancy and caregiver discrimination continue to limit the employment opportunities of women, and require enforcement and public education to equal employment opportunity in our nation's workplaces.

III. Conclusion: Closing the Gap – What's at Stake

Closing the pay gap is the right thing to do – but it is also an economic necessity. Closing the gap could have broad benefits for reducing poverty, growing the middle class and boosting our nation's economic growth. Economists widely agree that reducing inequality is a net economic positive – both in terms of the ability of individual workers to get better jobs at better pay, and in terms of the overall beneficial effect on our economy.

Discrimination imposes real costs on our economy – preventing our nation from fully enjoying the talents of all its workers, and unfairly limiting the employment and wage prospects for entire classes of people. In recent decades, increases in U.S. economic inequality have fallen disproportionately on women and minorities. For example, the declining value of the minimum wage has had a significant negative effect on women – who head one quarter of households with children.

Ultimately, the differences in pay for women and men compound over the years. According to an analysis by the Department of Labor's Chief Economist, by age 25, the average young woman working full time would have already earned $5,000 less over the course of her working career than the average 25-year old man. If that earnings gap is not corrected, by age 65, she will have lost hundreds of thousands of dollars over her working lifetime.[132] Fewer dollars for workers and their families means a real loss of economic security, at a time when no family can afford to be earning less.

Since the 1960s, women have moved into the paid labor force in record numbers. The share of women participating in the paid labor force has increased from 37.7 percent in 1960 to 57.7 percent in 2012. By 2012, female earners contributed to family income in 65 percent of the families with at least one wage earner. Among families with children, the share is even larger at 70 percent. Given the rising importance of women's earnings in family income, closing the pay gap is important to improving family outcomes, such as reducing the number of individuals, and especially children, who live in poverty.

What would happen to poverty rates if women's hourly wages were increased by 10 percent, an increase that still would not fully close the pay gap? In 2011, approximately 46.2 million individuals – including nearly 16 million children – were living in poverty. Raising all working women's wages by 10 percent would lift nearly 1.3 million individuals out of poverty, including more than half a million children.[133]

Reducing occupational segregation also is likely to benefit not only individual workers and their families, but the economy as a whole. Reducing inequality means that individual workers facing illegal barriers to good middle-class jobs or a fair paycheck will see personal gains in employment and wages. Improving the economic prospects of millions of American workers and their families will increase demand and boost job creation overall. Indeed, a recent paper by Hsieh, Hurst, Jones and Klenow (2013) finds that 15 to 20 percent of aggregate wage growth between 1960 and 2008 was due to a decline in barriers to occupational choice.[134] Employers also stand to benefit from a more equal society, as workers can be better matched to jobs and workplaces increase access to the diverse talent we need to help our companies compete in a 21st Century global economy.

Hard work should lead to a decent living for all Americans. Workers should know their worth and be empowered to claim it. Federal agencies should safeguard the right to equal pay and make certain all employers play by the same rules. Employers should share best practices for providing equal opportunity in the workplace. It should not take another fifty years to close the wage gap.

In marking Equal Pay Day this year, the President said, "[w]age inequality undermines the promise of fairness and opportunity upon which our country was founded." Fifty years after the Equal Pay Act's passage, we have taken important steps toward fulfilling that promise, but our journey is not complete. As we pause to honor this anniversary, we recommit ourselves to closing the gap – once and for all.

[1] U.S. Census Bureau. "Women's Earnings as a Percentage of Men's Earnings by Race and Hispanic Origin." *Historical Income Tables, Table P-40*. (2011). http://www.census.gov/hhes/www/income/data/historical/people/.

[2] Bureau of Labor Statistics, U.S. Department of Labor. "Employed persons by occupation, sex and age." *Current Population Survey*. (2013). http://www.bls.gov/cps/cpsaat09.htm.

[3] Bureau of Labor Statistics, U.S. Department of Labor. "Employment status of the civilian noninstitutional population by age, sex, and race." *Current Population Survey*. (2012). http://bls.gov/cps/cpsaat03.htm; Bureau of Labor Statistics, U.S. Department of Labor. "Labor Force Participation: 75 Years of Change, 1950-98, and 1998-2025." (1999). http://www.bls.gov/mlr/1999/12/art1full.pdf.

[4] U.S. Census Bureau. "Percentage of Managers who are women: 1940-2009." *Women in the Labor Force*. (2010). http://www.census.gov/newsroom/pdf/women_workforce_slides.pdf.

[5] U.S. Census Bureau. "Women's Earnings as a Percentage of Men's Earnings by Race and Hispanic Origin." *Historical Income Tables, Table P-40*. (2011). http://www.census.gov/hhes/www/income/data/historical/people/.

[6] National Center for Education Statistics, U.S. Department of Education. "Bachelor's, master's, and doctor's degrees conferred by degree-granting institutions, by sex of student and discipline division: 2010-2011." *Digest of Education Statistics*. http://nces.ed.gov/programs/digest/d12/tables/dt12_317.asp.

[7] Herman, A. M., & Castro, I. L. U.S. Department of Labor. "Equal Pay: A Thirty-Five Year Perspective." 62, Table 7. (1998).

[8] U.S. Census Bureau. "Census Bureau Reports Women-Owned Firms Numbered 7.8 Million in 2007, Generated Receipts of $1.2 Trillion." *Newsroom*. (2010). http://www.census.gov/newsroom/releases/archives/business_ownership/cb10-184.html.

[9] U.S. Census Bureau. "Census Bureau Reports Women-Owned Firms Numbered 7.8 Million in 2007, Generated Receipts of $1.2 Trillion." *Newsroom*. (2010). http://www.census.gov/newsroom/releases/archives/business_ownership/cb10-184.html.

[10] Herman, A. M., & Castro, I. L. U.S. Department of Labor. "Equal Pay: A Thirty-Five Year Perspective." 17. (1998).

[11] Bureau of Labor Statistics, U.S. Department of Labor. "Employed persons by detailed occupation and sex, 2012 annual averages." *Current Population Survey*. (2013). http://www.bls.gov/cps/cpsaat11.htm.

[12] Bureau of Labor Statistics, U.S. Department of Labor. "Women in the Labor Force: A Databook, 2012." *BLS Reports*. (2013). http://www.bls.gov/cps/wlf-databook-2012.pdf.

[13] Bureau of Labor Statistics, U.S. Department of Labor. "Women in the Labor Force: A Databook, 2012." *BLS Reports*. (2013). http://www.bls.gov/cps/wlf-databook-2012.pdf.

[14] Bureau of Labor Statistics, U.S. Department of Labor. "Median usual weekly earnings of full-time wage and salary workers, by sex, marital status, and presence and age of own children under 18 years old, 2011 annual averages." *Highlights of Women's Earnings in 2011*. 45. (2012) http://www.bls.gov/cps/cpswom2011.pdf.

[15] U.S. Census Bureau. "Income, Poverty, and Health Insurance Coverage in the United States: 2011," 48, Table A-4. (2012). http://www.census.gov/prod/2012pubs/p60-243.pdf.

[16] U.S. Census Bureau. "Income, Poverty, and Health Insurance Coverage in the United States: 2008." 36. (2009). http://www.census.gov/prod/2009pubs/p60-236.pdf.

[17] U.S. Census Bureau. "Full-time, year-round workers by median earnings and sex: 1960 to 2011." *Historical Income Tables*. http://www.census.gov/hhes/www/income/data/historical/people/.

[18] Lacey, T.A and Wright, B. "Employment Outlook: 2008-18, Occupational employment projections to 2018." *Monthly Labor Review, November 2009*. 82-123. (2008). www.bls.gov/opub/mlr/2009/11/art5full.pdf.

[19] Levitan, S.A & Belous, R.S. "Working wives and mothers: What happens to family life?" *Monthly Labor Review, September 1981*. 26-30. (1981). www.bls.gov/opub/mlr/1981/09/art4full.pdf.

[20] Bureau of Labor Statistics, U.S. Department of Labor. "Employment Characteristics of Families—2011." *BLS Reports*. (2012). http://www.bls.gov/news.release/famee.nr0.htm.

[21] Bureau of Labor Statistics, U.S. Department of Labor. "Median usual weekly earnings of full-time wage and salary workers, by detailed occupation and sex, 2011 annual averages." *Highlights of Women's Earnings in 2011*. Table 2. (2012). http://www.bls.gov/cps/cpswom2011.pdf.

[22] U.S. Bureau of Labor Statistics, U.S. Department of Labor. "Median usual weekly earnings of full-time wage and salary workers by occupation and sex, 1983 and 2000 annual averages." *Highlights of women's Earnings in 2000*. 8. (2000). http://bls.gov/cps/cpswom2000.pdf.

[23] U.S. Glass Ceiling Commission. "Glass Ceiling Commission: Good for Business Making Full Use of the Nation's Human Capitol." (March 1995). http://digitalcommons.ilr.cornell.edu/cgi/viewcontent.cgi?article=1118&context=key_workplace.

[24] Bureau of Labor Statistics, U.S. Department of Labor. "Median usual weekly earnings of full-time wage and salary workers, by detailed occupation and sex, 2011 annual averages." *Highlights of Women's Earnings in 2011*. Table 2. (2012). http://www.bls.gov/cps/cpswom2011.pdf.

[25] This included Members of Congress Florence Price Dwyer, Edith Green, Charles Goodell, Elizabeth Kee, Edna Kelly, Catherine May, Maurine Neuberger, Carlton Sickles, and Leonor K. Sullivan. Also in attendance were Vice President Lyndon B. Johnson, Assistant Labor Secretary and Director of the Women's Bureau Esther Peterson, former Women's Bureau Director Mary Anderson, and leaders from women's organizations and labor unions, including National Federation of Business and Professional Women President Dr. Minnie Miles, National Council of Negro Women President Dr. Dorothy Height, National Council of Jewish Women President Pearl Larner Willen, YWCA Director Ethlyn Christensen, United Auto Workers Women's Director Caroline Davis, AFL-CIO Legislative Director Andrew Biemiller, and General Federation of Women's Clubs Legislative Director Mary M. Chittenden.

[26] Kennedy, John F. "Remarks Upon Signing the Equal Pay Act." *The American Presidency Project*. (1963). http://www.presidency.ucsb.edu/ws/index.php?pid=9267.

[27] Bureau of Labor Statistics, U.S. Department of Labor. "Labor Force Participation: 75 Years of Change, 1950-98, and 1998-2025." (1999). http://www.bls.gov/mlr/1999/12/art1full.pdf.

[28] Harrison, Cynthia. "The Equal Pay Act of 1963: Compromise and Victory." *On Account of Sex: The Politics of Women's Issues 1945-1968*. 89-108. (1988).

[29] U.S. Government Printing Office. "American Women: Report of the President's Commission on the Status of Women (1963)."

[30] 110 Cong. Rec. 2577-2584 (1964).

[31] Goodman, B. & Wagner, P.M. "Makers: Women Who Make America." *Public Broadcasting System (PBS)*. (2013) http://www.pbs.org/makers/home/.

[32] Goodman, B. & Wagner, P.M. "Makers: Women Who Make America." *Public Broadcasting System (PBS)*. (2013) http://www.pbs.org/makers/home/.

[33] Frankel, M. *Tighter Rules on Job Prejudice Against Women Issued by U.S*, N.Y. Times, June 10, 1970.

[34] Herman, A. M., & Castro, I. L. U.S. Department of Labor. "Equal Pay: A Thirty-Five Year Perspective." 51. (1998).

[35] 29 CFR § 541.0.

[36] Equal Employment Opportunity Commission. "Timeline of Important EEOC Events." http://www.eeoc.gov/youth/history.html.

[37] Bureau of Labor Statistics, U.S. Department of Labor. "Labor Force Participation: 75 Years of Change, 1950-98, and 1998-2025." (1999). http://www.bls.gov/mlr/1999/12/art1full.pdf.

[38] Herman, A. M., & Castro, I. L. U.S. Department of Labor. "Equal Pay: A Thirty-Five Year Perspective." Appendix A, Table 1. (1998).

[39] Herman, A. M., & Castro, I. L. U.S. Department of Labor. "Equal Pay: A Thirty-Five Year Perspective." 19. (1998).

[40] Bureau of Labor Statistics, U.S. Department of Labor. "Labor force participation rates by sex, race, and Hispanic or Latino ethnicity, 1972-2009 annual averages." *Labor Force Characteristics by Race and ethnicity, 2009*. (2010). http://www.bls.gov/cps/cpsrace2009.pdf.

[41] B.I.G. Enterprises, Inc. and the Institute for Women's Policy Research. "An analysis of pay disparities between women and men by selected demographic characteristics, 1960 to 2010." *White Paper, Prepared for the U.S. Department of Labor, Women's Bureau*. (2012).

[42] Herman, A. M., & Castro, I. L. U.S. Department of Labor. "Equal Pay: A Thirty-Five Year Perspective." Appendix A, Table 2. (1998).

[43] Herman, A. M., & Castro, I. L. U.S. Department of Labor. "Equal Pay: A Thirty-Five Year Perspective." 19. (1998).

[44] Herman, A. M., & Castro, I. L. U.S. Department of Labor. "Equal Pay: A Thirty-Five Year Perspective." Appendix B, Table 1. (1998).

[45] Herman, A. M., & Castro, I. L. U.S. Department of Labor. "Equal Pay: A Thirty-Five Year Perspective." Appendix A, Table 3. (1998).

[46] U.S. Department of Labor. "Women's History/Our History: The Remarkable Bessie Margolin," *DOL News Brief, March 14, 2013*. http://www.dol.gov/_sec/newsletter/2013/20130314.htm; Schultz v. Wheaton Glass Co., 421 F.2d 259 (3d Cir. 1970), cert. denied 398 U.S. 905 (1970).

[47] Corning Glass Works v. Brennan, 417 U.S. 188 (1974).

[48] Herman, A. M., & Castro, I. L. U.S. Department of Labor. "Equal Pay: A Thirty-Five Year Perspective." 52. (1998).

[49] U.S. Census Bureau. "Income, Poverty, and Health Insurance Coverage in the United States: 2011." 48, Table A-4. (2012). http://www.census.gov/prod/2012pubs/p60-243.pdf.

[50] County of Washington v. Gunther, 452 U.S. 161 (1981).

[51] National Committee on Pay Equity. "Questions and Answers on Pay Equity." (2013). http://www.pay-equity.org/info-Q&A.html.

[52] Equal Employment Opportunity Commission. "Policy Guidance on Current Issues of Sexual Harassment." (1990). http://www.eeoc.gov/policy/docs/currentissues.html; Meritor Savings Bank v. Vinson, 477 U.S. 57 (1986).

[53] U.S. Department of Labor. "The Federal Glass Ceiling Commission, A Solid Investment: Making Full Use of the Nation's Human Capitol." (March 1985). http://www.dol.gov/oasam/programs/history/reich/reports/ceiling2.htm.

[54] U.S. Department of Labor. "Wage and Hour Division, The Family and Medical Leave Act Overview." (2013). http://www.dol.gov/whd/fmla/index.htm.

[55] National Center for Education Statistics, U.S. Department of Education. "Degrees Conferred by degree-granting institutions, by level of degree and sex of student: Selected years, 1869-70 through 2019-20." (2010). http://nces.ed.gov/pubs2011/2011015_3b.pdf.

[56] National Center for Education Statistics, U.S. Department of Education. "Degrees Conferred by degree-granting institutions, by level of degree and sex of student: Selected years, 1869-70 through 2019-20." (2010). http://nces.ed.gov/pubs2011/2011015_3b.pdf.

[57] Bureau of Labor Statistics, U.S. Department of Labor. "Median usual weekly earnings of full-time wage and salary workers 25 years and older, in constant (2011) dollars, by sex and educational attainment, 1979-2011 annual averages." *Highlights of Women's Earnings in 2011.* 67-68. (2012). http://www.bls.gov/cps/cpswom2011.pdf.

[58] Bureau of Labor Statistics, U.S. Department of Labor. "Median usual weekly earnings of full-time wage and salary workers 25 years and older, in constant (2011) dollars, by sex and educational attainment, 1979-2011 annual averages." *Highlights of Women's Earnings in 2011.* 60. (2012). http://www.bls.gov/cps/cpswom2011.pdf.

[59] Bureau of Labor Statistics, U.S. Department of Labor. "Median usual weekly earnings of full-time wage and salary workers 25 years and older, in constant (2011) dollars, by sex and educational attainment, 1979-2011 annual averages." *Highlights of Women's Earnings in 2011.* 67. (2012). http://www.bls.gov/cps/cpswom2011.pdf.

[60] Bureau of Labor Statistics, U.S. Department of Labor. "Civilian labor force participation rates by age, sex, race, and ethnicity, 1990, 2000, 2010, and projected 2020." (2012). http://www.bls.gov/emp/ep_table_303.htm.

[61] U.S. Census Bureau. "Employment status of women by marital status and presence and age of children: 1970 to 2009." (2012). http://www.census.gov/compendia/statab/2012/tables/12s0599.pdf.

[62] U.S. Census Bureau. "Employment status of women by marital status and presence and age of children: 1970 to 2009." (2012). http://www.census.gov/compendia/statab/2012/tables/12s0599.pdf.

[63] U.S. Census Bureau. "Civilian labor force- percent distribution by sex and age: 1980 to 2010." (2012). http://www.census.gov/compendia/statab/2012/tables/12s0592.pdf.

[64] Bureau of Labor Statistics, U.S. Department of Labor. "Contribution of wives' earnings to family income, 1970-2010." *Women in the Labor Force: A Databook.* 81. (2013). http://www.bls.gov/cps/wlf-databook-2012.pdf.

[65] Bureau of Labor Statistics, U.S. Department of Labor. "Wives who earn more than their husbands, 1987-2010." *Women in the Labor Force: A Databook.* 82. (2013). http://www.bls.gov/cps/wlf-databook-2012.pdf.

[66] U.S. Census Bureau. "Full-time, year-round workers by median earnings and sex: 1960 to 2011." *Historical Income Tables.* (2011) http://www.census.gov/hhes/www/income/data/historical/people/.

[67] U.S. Census Bureau. "Money income in the United States: 1996." (1997). https://www.census.gov/prod/3/97pubs/P60-197.PDF.

[68] U.S. Census Bureau. "Women's Earnings as a Percentage of Men's Earnings by Race and Hispanic Origin." *Historical Income Tables, Table P-40*. (2011). http://www.census.gov/hhes/www/income/data/historical/people/.

[69] U.S. Census Bureau. "Income, Poverty, and Health Insurance Coverage in the United States: 2011." 48, Table A-4. (2012). http://www.census.gov/prod/2012pubs/p60-243.pdf.

[70] Council of Economic Advisors, The White House. "Explaining Trends in the Gender Wage Gap." (1998). http://clinton4.nara.gov/WH/EOP/CEA/html/gendergap.html.

[71] U.S. Equal Employment Opportunity Commission. EEOC Notice No. 915.002. (October 29, 2007). http://www.eeoc.gov/policy/docs/coaches.html.

[72] Advisory Group of Women of Silicon Valley. "Unfinished Business: The Women in Silicon Valley Economy." *Collaborative Economics*. (April 2011). http://www.coecon.com/Reports/Archives/UnfinishedBusiness.pdf.

[73] National Center for Veterans Analysis and Statistics, U.S. Department of Veterans Affairs. *America's Women Veterans, Military Service History and VA Benefit Utilization Statistics.* (November 23, 2011). http://www.va.gov/VETDATA/docs/SpecialReports/Final_Womens_Report_3_2_12_v_7.pdf.

[74] National Center for Education Statistics, U.S. Department of Education. "Degrees Conferred by degree-granting institutions, by level of degree and sex of student: Selected years, 1869-70 through 2019-20." (2010). http://nces.ed.gov/pubs2011/2011015_3b.pdf.

[75] Bureau of Labor Statistics, U.S. Department of Labor. "Median usual weekly earnings of full-time wage and salary workers 25 years and over by sex, race, Hispanic or Latino ethnicity, and educational attainment, annual averages 1979-2011." (unpublished table).

[76] U.S. Census Bureau. "Income, poverty, and health insurance coverage in the United States: 2011." 48, Table A-4. (2012). http://www.census.gov/prod/2012pubs/p60-243.pdf.

[77] U.S. Census Bureau. "Educational Attainment--Full-Time, Year-Round Workers 25 Years Old and Over by Median Earnings and Sex: 1991 to 2011." *Historical Income Tables.* (2011). http://www.census.gov/hhes/www/income/data/historical/people/.

[78] U.S. Census Bureau. "Income, poverty, and health insurance coverage in the United states: 2011." 48, TABLE A-4. (2012). http://www.census.gov/prod/2012pubs/p60-243.pdf.

[79] Bureau of Labor Statistics, U.S. Department of Labor. "Civilian labor force participation rates by age, sex, race, and ethnicity, 1990, 2000, 2010, and projected 2020." (2012). http://www.bls.gov/emp/ep_table_303.htm.

[80] Bureau of Labor Statistics, U.S. Department of Labor. "Unpublished marital and family tables." *Current Population Survey.* 49, Table 3.

[81] Bureau of Labor Statistics, U.S. Department of Labor. "Employment status of the civilian noninstitutional population by sex, age, presence and age of youngest child, marital status, race, and Hispanic origin, March 2010." *Current Population Survey.* 25, Table 3. (2010).

[82] Bureau of Labor Statistics, U.S. Department of Labor. "Employment status of women by presence and age of youngest child, marital status, race, and Hispanic or Latino ethnicity, March 2010." *Women In the Labor Force: A Databook.* 15, Table 6. (2011). http://bls.gov/cps/wlf-databook-2011.pdf.

[83] U.S. Census Bureau. "Civilian Labor Force- Percent Distribution by sex and age: 1980 to 2010." (2012). http://www.census.gov/compendia/statab/2012/tables/12s0592.pdf.

[84] Bureau of Labor Statistics, U.S. Department of Labor. "Contribution of wives' earnings to family income, 1970-2010." *Women in the Labor Force: A Databook.* 81. (2013). http://www.bls.gov/cps/wlf-databook-2012.pdf.

[85] Bureau of Labor Statistics, U.S. Department of Labor. "Wives who earn more than their husbands." *Women in the Labor Force: A Databook.* 82. (2013). http://www.bls.gov/cps/wlf-databook-2012.pdf.

[86] Equal Employment Opportunity Commission. "Equal Pay Act Charges (includes concurrent charges with Title VII, ADEA and ADA) FY 1997- FY 2012." (2013). http://www.eeoc.gov/eeoc/statistics/enforcement/epa.cfm.

[87] Bureau of Labor Statistics, U.S. Department of Labor. "More Couples are Working Longer," *Working in the 21st Century: Chartbook.* (2013). http://www.bls.gov/opub/working/page17b.htm.

[88] Equal Employment Opportunity Commission. "Employer Best Practices for Workers With Caregiving Responsibilities." (2007). http://www.eeoc.gov/policy/docs/caregiver-best-practices.html.

[89] Ledbetter v. Goodyear Tire & Rubber Co., 550 U.S. 618 (2007).

[90] *TAP Talks with Lilly Ledbetter*. The American Prospect, April 23, 2008. http://www.prospect.org/cs/articles?article=tap_talks_with_lilly_ledbetter.

[91] National Equal Pay Enforcement Task Force. "National Equal Pay Enforcement Task Force." *The White House.* . (2010). http://www.whitehouse.gov/sites/default/files/rss_viewer/equal_pay_task_force.pdf.

[92] In 2010, women on average earned 81 cents for every dollar earned by a man. Bureau of Labor Statistics, U.S. Department of Labor. *Women at Work.* (2011). In 2011 and 2012, that figure fluctuated between 80 and 82 cents. Bureau of Labor Statistics, U.S. Department of Labor. "Labor Force Statistics from Current Population Survey." *Current Population Survey.* http://www.bls.gov/cps/earnings.htm#demographics; Updated quarterly CPS earnings figures by demographics by quarter through the end of 2012 *available at* http://www.bls.gov/news.release/wkyeng.t01.htm.

[93] U.S. Census Bureau. "Income, Poverty and Health Insurance Coverage in the United States." *Current Population Reports 2011.* (Sept. 2012). http://www.census.gov/prod/2012pubs/p60-243.pdf.

[94] Calculated from Bureau of Labor Statistics CPS data, *available at* http://www.bls.gov/cps/cpsrace2011.pdf.

[95] A March 2011 White House report entitled "Women in America: Indicators of Social and Economic Well-Being," found that while earnings for women and men typically increase with higher levels of education, male-female pay gap persists at all levels of education for full-time workers (35 or more hours per week), according to 2009 Bureau of Labor Statistics wage data. Potentially non-discriminatory factors can explain some of the gender wage differences. Even so, after controlling for differences in skills and job characteristics, women still earn less than men. Council of Economic Advisors. "Explaining Trends in the Gender Wage Gap." (June 1998); *see also,* Hegewisch, A., Williams, C., Harbin, V. *The Gender Wage Gap by Occupation.* (2012). (women's median earnings less than men in virtually all occupations); LoSasso, A. T., et al. "The $16,819 Pay Gap For Newly Trained Physicians: The Unexplained Trend Of Men Earning More Than Women." *30 Health Affairs 193.* (2011). Ultimately, the research literature still finds an unexplained gap exists even after accounting for potential explanations, and finds that the narrowing of the pay gap for women has slowed since the 1980s. Jacobsen, J.P. *The Economics of Gender.* 44. (2007); Blau, F.D. & Kahn, L.M. "The U.S. gender pay gap in the 1990s: slowing convergence." *60 Industrial and Labor Relations Review 45.* (2006). In addition to the gender pay gap, scholars have found race and ethnicity-based pay gaps that put workers of color at a disadvantage. Altonji, J.G. and Blank, R. M. "Race and Gender in the Labor Market," in *Handbook of Labor Economics* (Ashenfelter, O. and Card, D., eds.). 3143. (1999).

[96] Bureau of Labor Statistics, U.S. Department of Labor. "Women in the Labor Force: A Databook" *BLS Reports.* 12-13, Table 3. (2013). http://www.bls.gov/cps/wlf-databook-2012.pdf.

[97] Bureau of Labor Statistics, U.S. Department of Labor. "Women in the Labor Force: A Databook" *BLS Reports.* 1; 13-15, Table 4. (2013). http://www.bls.gov/cps/wlf-databook-2012.pdf.

[98] National Center for Education Statistics, U.S. Department of Education. "Bachelor's, master's, and doctor's degrees conferred by degree-granting institutions, by sex of student and discipline division: 2009-10." U.S. *Digest of Education Statistics.* Table 290. (2011). http://nces.ed.gov/programs/digest/d11/tables/dt11_290.asp.

[99] Bureau of Labor Statistics, U.S. Department of Labor. "Women in the Labor Force: A Databook, 2012." *BLS Reports.* (2013). http://www.bls.gov/cps/wlf-databook-2012.pdf.

[100] Goldin, C. *Understanding the Gender Gap: An Economic History of American Women* (1990).

[101] CEA calculations based on Current Population Survey.

[102] Women's Bureau, U.S. Department of Labor. "20 Leading Occupations of Employed Women, 2010." (2010). http://www.dol.gov/wb/factsheets/20lead2010.htm.

[103] Women's Bureau, U.S. Department of Labor. "Nontraditional Occupations of Employed Women in 2010." (2010). http://www.dol.gov/wb/stats/NontraJobs_2010.htm.

[104] Herman, A. M., & Castro, I. L. U.S. Department of Labor. "Equal Pay: A Thirty-Five Year Perspective." 18. (1998).

[105] Blau, F.D., Brummund, P. and Yung-Hsu Liu, A. "Trends in Occupational Segregation by Gender 1970-2009: Adjusting for the Impact of Changes in the Occupational Coding System." *NBER Working Paper.* (2012).

[106] U.S. Department of Commerce, Economics and Statistics Administration. "Women in STEM: A Gender Gap to Innovation." (August 2011).

[107] U.S. Department of Veterans Affairs. "America's Women: Past, Present and Future, (2007)." http://www.va.gov/VETDATA/docs/SpecialReports/Womenveterans_Past_Present_Future_9-30-07a.pdf.

[108] U.S. Census Bureau. "Facts for Features: Women's History Month." *Newsroom.* (2013). *http://www.census.gov/newsroom/releases/archives/facts_for_features_special_editions/cb13-ff04.html*.

[109] Alliance for National Defense. "Women in Combat." *Issue Paper.* http://www.4militarywomen.org/Women_in_Combat.htm.

[110] Becker, G. *The Economics of Discrimination.* (1957); Goldin, C. "A Pollution Theory of Discrimination: Male and Female Differences in Occupations and Earnings." *NBER Working Paper.* (2002).

[111] Mincer, J. and Polachek, S. "Family Investments in Human Capital: Earnings of Women." *Journal of Political Economy* 82:2. (1974).

[112] Blau, F.D., Ferber, M.A., Winkler, A.E. *The Economics of Women, Men, and Work (6th Edition).* (2010).

[113] Weinberger, Catherine J. "An Economist's Perspective on Women in the IT Workforce." *Encyclopedia of Gender and Information Technology, Information Science Publishing (Idea Group).* (2006).

[114] Hunt, J. "Why do Women Leave Science and Engineering?" *NBER Working Paper.* (2010).

[115] U.S. Bureau of Labor Statistics, U.S. Department of Labor. "Employed persons by occupation, sex and age." *Current Population Survey.* (2013). http://www.bls.gov/cps/cpsaat09.htm.

[116] Institute for Women's Policy Research. "New Study: Men Earn More Than Women Within Nearly All the Most Common Occupations." (2012). http://www.iwpr.org/press-room/press-releases/new-study-men-earn-more-than-women-within-nearly-all-the-most-common-occupations. In a recent review of 2010 Census data, Bloomberg found only one of 285 major occupations where women's median pay was higher than that of men – personal care and service workers. Bass, F. Shining Shoes Best Way Wall Street Women Outearn Men, Bloomberg. (Mar. 16, 2012). *Available at* http://www.bloomberg.com/news/2012-03-16/shining-shoes-best-way-wall-street-women-outearn-men.html

[117] LoSasso, A. T., et al. "The $16,819 Pay Gap For Newly Trained Physicians: The Unexplained Trend Of Men Earning More Than Women." *30 Health Affairs 193.* (2011). *Available at* http://content.healthaffairs.org/content/30/2/193.abstract. Catalyst also reviewed 2011 government data showing a gender pay gap for women lawyers, and that data confirms that the gap exists for a range of professional and technical occupations. Bureau of Labor Statistics, U.S. Department of Labor. "Median weekly earnings of full-time wage and salary workers by detailed occupation and sex." (2012). http://www.bls.gov/cps/cpsaat39.pdf.

[118] Bureau of Labor Statistics, U.S. Department of Labor. "Median weekly earnings of full-time wage and salary workers by detailed occupation and sex." (2012). http://www.bls.gov/cps/cpsaat39.pdf; LoSasso, A. T., et al. "The $16,819 Pay Gap For Newly Trained Physicians: The Unexplained Trend Of Men Earning More Than Women." *30 Health Affairs 193.* (2011). *Available at* http://content.healthaffairs.org/content/30/2/193.abstract.

[119] Benard, S., Paik, I., and Correll, S. J. "Cognitive Bias and the Motherhood Penalty." *59 Hastings L.J. 1359.* (2007-2008); Benard, S., Paik, I., and Correll, S. J. "Getting a Job: Is There a Motherhood Penalty?" 112 *Am. J. of Sociology 5.* (March 2007). http://gender.stanford.edu/sites/default/files/motherhoodpenalty.pdf.

[120] Office of the Press Secretary. "Remarks by the President in the State of the Union Address." *The White House.* (2010). http://www.whitehouse.gov/the-press-office/remarks-president-state-union-address.

[121] These include Title VII of the Civil Rights Act of 1964 (enforced by the EEOC, DOJ and OPM), the Equal Pay Act (enforced by EEOC and OPM), and Executive Order 11246 (enforced by DOL).

[122] Sutphen, M. "Putting Washington at the Service of the Middle Class." *The White House Rural Council.* (2010). http://www.whitehouse.gov/blog/2010/01/27/putting-washington-service-middle-class.

[123] National Equal Pay Enforcement Task Force. "National Equal Pay Enforcement Task Force." *The White House.* (2010). http://www.whitehouse.gov/sites/default/files/rss_viewer/equal_pay_task_force.pdf.

[124] Office of the Vice President. "Vice President Biden Holds Middle Class Task Force Event on Work and Family." *The White House.* (2010). http://www.whitehouse.gov/the-press-office/vice-president-biden-holds-middle-class-task-force-event-work-and-family.

[125] Both the Notice of Rescission and the new guidance information can be found at http:www.dol.gov/ofccp/compguidance.

[126] Division of Behavioral and Social Sciences and Education. "Measuring and Collecting Pay Information from U.S. Employers by Gender, Race, and National Origin" *The National Academies.* (2010). http://www8.nationalacademies.org/cp/projectview.aspx?key=49344.

[127] The National Acadamies Press. "Collecting Compensation Data from Employers." *National Acadamies of Sciences.* (2012). http://www.nap.edu/catalog.php?record_id=13496.

[128] 76 Fed. Reg. 49398 (Aug. 10, 2011).

[129] U.S. Department of Labor. "Equal Pay." (2012). http://www.dol.gov/equalpay/

[130] The Women's Bureau, U.S. Department of Labor. "Equal Pay App Challenge: Final Results and Prize Winners." (2012). http://www.dol.gov/equalpay/apps-winners.htm.

[131] The White House. "Accomplishments of the Equal Pay Task Force: Fighting for Fair Pay in the Workplace." (April 2012). www.whitehouse.gov/...equal_pay_taskforce.pdf.

[132] White House Council on Women and Girls,."The Key to an Economy Built to Last." (April 2012). http://www.whitehouse.gov/sites/default/files/email-files/womens_report_final_for_print.pdf.

[133] See Appendix for methods used to calculate new poverty figures.

[134] Hsieh, C., Hurst, E. Jones, C. I., Klenow, P. J. "The Allocation of Talent and U.S. Economic Growth." *NBER Working Paper.* (2013).

Appendix: Methods Used to Compute New Poverty Rates

To simulate what would happen if we increased female earnings, we used data from the 2012 March Annual Social and Economic Supplement to the Current Population Survey (CPS). Using the same poverty universe incorporated by the Census Bureau (http://www.census.gov/prod/2012pubs/p60-243.pdf), we increased the annual earnings of working women age 18 and over by 10 percent. Doing so would lift nearly 1.3 million individuals out of poverty (Table A1, column 5). It would also lift more than 700,000 people out of poverty who live in single female-headed families with children. About 550,000 children would be brought out of poverty under such an exercise, with over 400,000 children coming from families with single mothers.

Table A1: Individuals and Children in Poverty Before and After Increasing Female Earnings 10% (Number in Thousands)

	Original		New		Difference	
	Number in Poverty	Percent	Number in Poverty	Percent	Number	Percent
Individuals						
Total Individuals	46,247	15.0	44,952	14.6	1,295	0.4
Individuals in Families with Children						
Under 18	27,505	18.5	26,535	17.8	969	0.7
Female Reference Person Family	15,193	42.7	14,460	40.7	733	2.1
Husband-Wife Family	10,434	9.9	10,203	9.7	231	0.2
Individuals in Families with No						
Children Under 18	18,742	11.8	18,417	11.6	325,735	0.2
Children						
Children in Families with Children						
Under 18	15,963	21.7	15,416	21.0	547	0.7
Female Reference Person Family	9,525	46.2	9,086	44.1	440	2.1
Husband-Wife Family	5,320	11.0	5,214	10.8	106	0.2

Note: Families include related and unrelated subfamilies

Source: Current Population Survey, March 2012

45

www.ingramcontent.com/pod-product-compliance
Lightning Source LLC
Chambersburg PA
CBHW050834180526
45159CB00004B/1904